757
reward

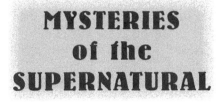

MYSTERIES
of the
SUPERNATURAL

In *Mysteries of the Supernatural*, Darrin is gifting the reader with information and skills for relating to other invisible forms of life that interpenetrate and share our world . . . our lives with us. He opens the gates of his experience and knowledge so we may respectfully, and with discernment, relate to the host of invisible neighbors that populate the "in-scape" of our world's landscape. As a sort of "outreach and education minister for the invisibles," I applaud this book and look forward to more!

—Orion Foxwood
Author of *The Candle and the Crossroads:*
A Book of Appalachian Conjure and Southern Root Work

I finished Darrin's new book and I love it! It's like a breath of fresh air to see a writer caution folks about running willy-nilly with spirits. It was easy to read and I learned some new things, too. Darrin has done a wonderful job in writing a book that will help folks move forward in their own growth. I could feel my southern culture within the pages. I love the stories, they put you right there!

—Starr Casas,
Author of *The Conjure Workbook Vol. 1: Working the Root*

All my life I've been curious about the unknown, which is why I got involved in paranormal investigating. With Darrin's book, I can now use the information he shared to help me become a better person spiritually and to understand the spiritual world around us. Everything you ever wanted to know about the supernatural is in this book, thanks Darrin!

—Rhonda Burton
Arkansas Ghost Catchers

Darrin is a master storyteller and teacher. *Mysteries of the Supernatural* is an illuminating look into unexplained shadows!

—Travis Sanders
Star of A&E's *Psychic Kids: Children of the Paranormal*

MYSTERIES
of the
SUPERNATURAL

A Psychic's Guide beyond the Veil

DARRIN WILLIAM OWENS

4th Dimension Press ■ Virginia Beach ■ Virginia

4th Dimension Press
215 67th Street
Virginia Beach, VA 23451-2061

ISBN 13: 978-0-87604-771-2

Cover design by Christine Fulcher

"*Pleasure to me is wonder—the unexplored, the unexpected, the thing that is hidden and the changeless thing that lurks behind superficial mutability. To trace the remote in the immediate; the eternal in the ephemeral; the past in the present; the infinite in the finite; these are to me the springs of delight and beauty.*"

—H.P. Lovecraft

Table of Contents

Acknowledgments

First and foremost, I want to thank my guardian angels at Edgar Cayce's A.R.E. for their creative magic, love, and support: Jennie Taylor Martin, Cassie McQuagge, Susan Lendvay, and Mary Warren Pinnell—I love you!

To my partner and soul mate, Robin Branscum: you amaze me every day with the love and support you give me. You are the Divine's greatest gift in my life.

To Carol Johnson: a lifelong friend, and an amazing assistant, what would I do without you?

To my spiritual Mother and dear friend, Helen Reddy: I'm blessed by your love and friendship.

To Rosemary Ellen Guiley: thank you for helping me lift the veil even more and for guiding me on how to soften my soapbox with certain psychic avenues. Your supernatural blessing is a true honor and gift in my life. I love you very much!

To Momma Starr and Orion Foxwood: you don't know how much you have graced my life with your writings and your wisdom. My remembrance of and my reconnection with my ancestral power happened because of you.

To Rhonda Burton, founder of Arkansas Ghost Catchers: your friendship is so important in my life, and your work with the Paranormal Realm is essential. Keep the light going, girlfriend!

And to my readers, clients, and fans all over the world: you folks rock! I love you.

Foreword

Foreword by **Rosemary Ellen Guiley**

There are three ways that people are inspired to probe into the paranormal and metaphysical realms. One is having an awareness of the unseen from earliest memories. Darrin W. Owens is such a person, born with a gift to see and experience beings and phenomena that pass by most people.

The second is through having a personal experience that one cannot explain rationally according to what is considered "ordinary reality." Often these experiences rock a person's world and even turn it upside down, blowing away all preconceived beliefs. Many people are drawn into the field in this manner.

The third is curiosity that has been piqued by television, films, books—our pop-culture—and the experiences of those we know.

In all three cases, when people are motivated to a new search for truth, they need solid information to help them find their way. In *Mysteries of the Supernatural: A Psychic's Guide beyond the Veil,* Darrin has written one of the finest guides to date for the spiritual seeker, the curious, and the experienced explorers of other realms. He covers every base important to the quest, whether it is pursuit of paranormal phenomena or experiences with the dead and with beings in other realms. Even more important, he tackles the dark side as well as the light side.

In my own thirty-plus years of researching and investigating the paranormal and metaphysical fields, I have always advocated getting a grounding in as many subjects as possible. Like Darrin, I had experiences from an early age, which I took for granted as reality for everyone. As I got older, I soon realized that awareness of non-physical realities are not readily available to all, and that experiences have common ground but a great deal of personalized subjectivity to them. I realized how deeply interconnected are all the phenomena and experiences. And, I realized how important it is to have knowledge of both sides of the fence—the good and benevolent, and the bad and malevolent. Sooner or later, the seeker encounters both.

Thus, the good seeker needs a broad base of knowledge. I have always said that no matter where you enter the Path, be it ghosts or angels or ETs or something else, if you stay on the Path long enough and go deep enough, you will see the interconnectivity and realize the importance of a broad education. The realms beyond the physical have no sharp boundaries, but overlap and even seep into each other.

Discernment becomes a crucial skill in navigating these realms and validating experiences and communications of all kinds. Without knowledge and experience, there is little, if any, discernment. Darrin's fine guide will help you learn solid basics and fill in the blanks of your education.

I am often asked by those new to the paranormal, "Where is all this going?" "What am I supposed to do with it?" Stepping onto the Path is a quest and a journey, and usually we do not know where exactly we will go. But if we have discernment, an open mind, fearlessness, and trust in good guidance, the journey unfolds in a meaningful, purposeful way. The journey is different for everyone, even though we share the Path with others.

Darrin makes the point that the veil between realms is opening at an increasing pace, with impetus from both sides. We are increasingly drawn (or even plunged) into experience, and the beings in other realms are increasingly drawn to interact with us, some for better, some for worse. I have found this to be the case in my own work as well. The "interdimensional earth" is already the new reality, and those of us who take time to study will be prepared to meet the challenges of living in it. It's actually quite exciting—we are all pioneers pushing out new frontiers!

I have long admired Darrin's work and the integrity he brings to it. He tells it as he sees it and knows it, from his own experience and careful research. This book will stand the test of time, a classic in the literature of the field. What's more, Darrin brings a delightful sense of humor to it all. You'll enjoy reading this book—it's fun as well as profound. It is truly a handbook for visionary living, the focal point of my own work as well.

Mysteries of the Supernatural is now on my Essential Reading list, and I recommend this book as an excellent, well-rounded guide for both beginners and the experienced. There is always something new to be found around the next bend, and you'll reach for this book again and again.

Rosemary Ellen Guiley
Author and President of Visionary Living, Inc.

Introduction

We live in the midst of invisible forces whose effects alone we perceive. We move among invisible forms whose actions we very often do not perceive at all, though we may be profoundly affected by them.   (Dion Fortune, *Psychic-Self Defense* [San Francisco: Weiser Books, 1930], 3)

Working as a professional psychic and paranormal researcher for over eighteen years, I have had the great privilege of delving into many adventures with the supernatural. It seems that when people are born with a high psychic awareness, they are almost transfixed between two worlds from the very beginning. My entire childhood was like that. Living between two realms was normal for me. In essence, the supernatural was natural. Throughout the years of living a psychic's life, I began to pay closer attention to the expanded awareness of other dimensions that vibrated all around me. Many of us have had this same realization only to have it chalked up to a wild imagination. I have come to believe that as children, the "monster" in the closet or our imaginary playmates may not be far from being real manifestations of the supernatural world. Just recently, I discovered a word that I have adopted for myself that seems to fit me perfectly, and it is "supernaturalist." The term "supernaturalist" is not a word that you hear very often. When pronounced aloud, it rings with a very cool and mysterious tone. The *Collins English Dictionary* sums up the meaning of this elusive label the best as "a person who believes in supernatural forces or agencies as producing effects in this world" or "characterized by a belief in supernatural forces or agencies as producing effects in this world."

In general we can look at the supernatural as the manifestation of the unearthly, weird, and miraculous, while a supernaturalist lives in constant awareness of its elusive presence. The definitions of supernaturalist mention that the supernatural realms actually produce effects. Experiencing the effects is very much the case in my work. I'm seeing, especially during the past few years, the veil between our physical world and the supernatural worlds thinning at an alarming rate. In fact, these otherworldly dimensions are affecting us by the actions being taken on both sides to lift the curtain to see what's there! Not only are we curious, but the beings, entities, and supernatural creatures on the "other side" are also curious about our world. We can see this curiosity take shape by the many eyewitness accounts of odd occurrences experienced by thousands of people worldwide. The stories are countless and have hit the media like a cyclone. I can always tell when something is changing in the global brain by watching it reflected in our current popular culture. You can definitely see this reflection in the outpouring of the prevailing paranormal and supernatural television shows.

I'm going to be kind and pass over disclaiming the ridiculous paranormal reality shows of exploitation. Instead, I will mention two prominent and well-made television series in order to make my point. In 1993, a groundbreaking TV series called *The X-Files* exploded into our media consciousness. The show's focus centered on two FBI agents as they investigated matters of the strange and unknown—mostly unidentified flying objects (UFOs) and extraterrestrials (ETs).

During the 1990s, I noticed a great surge of interest regarding the affirmation that *The X-Files* founded itself on, "The Truth is Out There." Suddenly we had a great need to know more about supernatural matters as we began to ask ourselves, "Is there life and intelligence out there?" Again, this search was not new to the planet, but during the past twenty years with our evolution of technology and media outlets, the supernatural has spread far and wide like never before. In the nineties, the global mind that was reflected in popular culture continued to maintain an arm's length with anything paranormal or otherworldly as something "out there" to be discovered. It was still regarded as science fiction or fantasy, which might or might not be real.

At this point, let's jet into the future about twelve years and talk about my personal favorite television series, *Supernatural*. Fitting, don't you think? In 2005, I remember the time and the place when I first watched the pilot episode of *Supernatural* as though it were yesterday. I was at my home in Arkansas and just happened to flip the TV to a random channel since nothing else was catching my interest. I was immediately captivated by the story line of two brothers who were raised to fight and exorcise demons and help as many people afflicted with supernatural disturbances as possible. Over time and as I watched the show regularly, I realized that as the global mind was progressing, we were allowing more of the truth to surface. The idea was not so much in understanding the truth as being "out there" but realizing that the truth is living and breathing with us, right here in our own back yard. The *Supernatural* television series reflected just that concept. Not only did the brothers battle demons, but they also dealt with an array of supernatural creatures—all the way from ghosts and fairies to angels and pagan gods. And it was all due to that fact that the veil between our world and the supernatural world was becoming easily passable. We are, without a shadow of any doubt, becoming more aware that we co-exist with beings that are not of this physical plane. And as popular culture reflects to us so well, I am seeing the very same thing in my work as a psychic and as a "supernaturalist." Let me mention here that I realize these accuracies are not as dramatic as Hollywood wants to portray, but I believe there is a very clear mirror of growth with the supernatural realms that can be seen in these two current television series. I can safely say that the *truth* is not *out there*. It's *right here*.

So what do these notions mean? What is the significance for our planet and our spiritual evolution? It's simple. Opening our minds to the realization that our planet and universe are not all that exist is one of the most enlightening ideas we can discover. As we evolve spiritually and psychically, we progress closer and closer to higher abilities of peering beyond the illusory, spectral veil that separates our world from the supernatural realms. We are moving beyond merely seeing orbs and ghosts! We are evolving our psychic perception enough to be able to see beings and intelligences that have existed beyond Avalon's mists for many centuries. The Paranormal Realm is just one of several realms within the supernatural. Below is a list of the realms within the supernatural that I have compiled over the years from my research and psychic work. I have been blessed to have been given the gift of traveling within these realms, sometimes on purpose and sometimes via a shocking "falling down the rabbit hole" experience.

The 7 Supernatural Realms

- The Dark Realm: Demonic Beings and Fallen Angels
- The Nature Realm: Earth Folk and Nature Spirits
- The Multidimensional Realm: UFOs and Cryptid Creatures
- The Paranormal Realm: Ghosts and Hauntings
- The Spiritual Realm: Human Souls and Spirit Guides
- The Divine Realm: Gods, Goddesses, and Angelic Beings
- The Source Realm: Mother/Father God: Source of all Creation

In my previous book, *Becoming Masters of Light*, for the first time I wrote about my work as a practicing exorcist. This specific gift has given me the ability to literally discern and perceive different realities within the veil as well as to access information and navigate freely among the realms listed above. Also, in doing the work of exorcism in my paranormal research with clients, I have encountered many different energies and beings trying to make their way into our world. For some supernatural beings, it's as easy as using unlimited thought to pass between realms, while other beings seem to catch our attention in some form or fashion.

Some of these beings need a hook from our world to grab our notice and then slide right on over into our realm. This circumstance explains the reality of possession. Some of these supernatural beings—mostly lost souls and demonic beings—vibrate at a very low level of energy. In order to be congruent with the vibration of the earth plane, they need a host. Guess who? Yes, us! Possession is why I stress the importance of spiritual empowerment and well-being, which promote the absence of any mental or emotional hooks for nonhuman entities to feed on. These particular energies feed off fear and, with no real logic, want to create and feed more fear. As a sensitive person with the gift of exorcism, this realm is one that I have had to become very familiar with. Some may see this shadow reality from time to time, but for those of us who are gatekeepers between realms, we know the modus operandi of the Dark Realm all too well. You may not think that this is a gift worth having, but it is quite the opposite. Because of my understanding of this particular realm, I have helped many individuals clear their energy and release themselves from its grip. It does take strong faith, discernment, and spiritual power to maneuver there, and that's a fact. I'll write more about this process in the chapter about the Dark Realm.

On the other side of the coin, we have as another example the Divine Realm. Here we are blessed by the presence of angelic beings, archangels, saints, and ascended masters. Currently, many people are psychically opening up very strongly to this realm. Over that past twenty years, there have been great achievements in the writings and teachings of angelology and the wisdom of the masters. Again, it is just a reflection of where the global mind is journeying on the intuitive level.

Another quick example is the Paranormal Realm. This realm has actually become somewhat of an obsession with popular culture. Everywhere you look, there are new paranormal reality shows on television. Yet another celebrity medium or psychic appears on a talk show and discusses his or her gift.

Ghost hunting groups are like the plague, saturating the Paranormal Realm with their ghost hunting kits, flashlights, and EVP/EMF detectors. Amateurs! I can easily climb on a soapbox about this subject. The exploitations of the Paranormal Realm by some people are sickening. It should not be for entertainment purposes only; I don't care what the "Syfy" (Science Fiction) channel believes. But, looking at paranormal groups and TV shows from a different point of view and seeing them through the perspective of the global mind, I can recognize that their popularity is yet another reflection of where we are growing inwardly. Remember, our pop culture will give us away every time. The Paranormal Realm is a very illusory arena in which its inhabitants are the lost souls (ghosts) and poltergeists, just to name a few. This one seems to be a realm that hovers between our world and the Spiritual Realm. It's a kind of hallway or house for souls. It also seems to be the realm that has become the most accessible and popular to connect with. I'll go into more detail on the subject later in this book.

There are many psychics who have many different abilities. Some can connect with one or more of these realms. Mediums seem to connect mainly with the Paranormal Realm and the Spiritual Realm, therefore having access to lost loved ones and information from the "other side."

In my research I have noticed certain tiered levels to the realms. A few levels can flow in and out of the other, and please remember that we are talking about the supernatural here. To try to box it up with tidy labels is rather silly, but I'm going to try to explain it to you as I have experienced it over the years. At the bottom of the levels is, of course, the Dark Realm. This lower level may explain to some degree our deep-seated belief that the archetypal "hell" is below us. The Dark Realm is the densest of the realms and contains no divine light at all. It's a realm where all of the concentrated negative energies such as demonic beings, fallen angels, and any beings with fear as their main intent reside.

Next, we move up to the Nature Realm. Yes, you guessed it; fairies, elves, gnomes, and other nature folk live here. They seem to be the guardians and the gatekeepers of nature. Contrary to popular belief, these archetypal earth beings really have no interest in conversing much with humans anymore. As a matter of fact, they can become downright snippy if you happen to trip into their realm. Their main intent is to keep the balance of nature, and humans don't seem to be falling in line with that balance very well. These beings are not really pure love or pure fear. They are indifferent, you might say. I'll write more about these little critters later.

Then we move into the Multidimensional Realm. This is a realm that is quite intriguing. I have filed everything from Bigfoot, the Mothman, and Shadow People to UFOs in this realm. They all seem to exhibit a multidimensional presence in their nature. I know that most people will agree with me that UFOs are multidimensional, but why Bigfoot? It's simple; some of the cryptic creatures like Bigfoot and the Mothman seem to be able to travel easily between realms and dimensions. This is not a question when we think of ETs, but have you ever considered that we have our own multidimensional beings living right here on earth? I'll detail this idea more in the coming chapters, but this realm is one that we are still discovering and about which I'm very eager to continue investigating. Some of these beings seem to vibrate to love, but others in this realm seem to have an unknown agenda. Fascinating!

After this realm, we journey to the Paranormal Realm and then to the Spiritual Realm.

The Spiritual Realm is where we human souls go when we pass through the tunnel of light to the other side. It's our home away from earth, so to speak, and it's where we learn and grow in awareness of our spiritual nature. An interesting note is that in my work I have discovered that the tunnel of light after death is a protective sheath that continues into the Spiritual Realm. This tunnel actually blankets us on our journey home. When a soul chooses, for whatever reason, to ignore the light, it is then pushed away and becomes stuck in the Paranormal Realm, heavy and earthbound. This absence of light is the experience of a lost soul or ghosts. The Spiritual Realm is also where we connect with our spiritual guides. Some trance channels spend a lot of time here, directing their psychic focus on communication with their guides.

Next is the Divine Realm. Human souls catch glimpses of this realm from time to time. Those individuals we call saints and mystics inhabit the Divine Realm. Devoted souls such as the Master Jesus, Buddha, and Saint Padre Pio were given a type of Jacob's ladder to this realm. As master teachers, it was their mission to bring the wisdom teachings of this realm to our realm on earth. All of the master teachers, saints, and the archetypal gods and goddesses reside here. The angelic beings and archangels also call the Divine Realm their home. This realm is the closest to the Source, that of all creative power.

The last realm is that of the Source. This realm is comprised of pure Divine Love Consciousness. This is the realm of Mother/Father God. It is the realm of consciousness to which all souls will eventually return. Our psychic sight must be focused on this realm at all times. All healing, discernment, and our higher selves are directly linked to the Source Realm. No one has entered this realm except the angelic beings created by the Source.

Those in the Divine Realm are well on their way to Divine Love Consciousness, and one day we will be, too. That's why we have an encoded divinity within us called the "Soul." This Soul, which is linked to the Divine Realm, bypasses all the rest because holiness is our true nature. If we remain linked to our divinity, then we can safely navigate the worldly dimensions without attachment and without becoming stuck. The purpose of my book is to help souls become aware of their supernatural surroundings and to strengthen their spiritual power with the realization of that awareness. I have added many tools in this work to help you become aware of these realms around you. My goal is for you to remain protected and comfortable as the portals open more and more to your own psychic and spiritual evolution. Knowledge is power, and knowledge abolishes fear.

With this new book, I also hope to soften the fear and excitement that surrounds the Supernatural Realm while revealing it as a normal occurrence in the universe. We are being asked to broaden our perceptual horizons on this planet. The "unveiling" is forcing us to open our mind's multidimensional eyes wider to see these paranormal realities not so much as something to be feared but as new ways of seeing life. We are multisensory beings living among multidimensional realities. It's time to explore and discover these new territories of spiritual and psychic mystery.

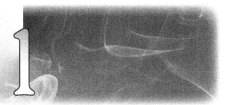

Supernatural Crossroads: The Threshold between the Seen and the Unseen

(A Special Note to the Reader)

The crossroads, a place where two roads intersect, is the subject of many religious and old-fashioned folk belief systems worldwide. In my neighborhood, most crossroads are outside the borders of a town or intertwined in deep hollows in the countryside. These locations are often considered to be supernatural. As a child, I lived near a crossroads. There were two well-worn dirt roads that crossed each other, smack-dab in the woods. I was a country kid, and we lived in the boonies. When I disappeared, my mother would always go looking for me at the crossroads. There I was, sitting right in the middle of it. Even then, I must have realized there was power there, a thinning place of the veil between worlds. I believe there is a crossroads for every realm of the supernatural.

The crossroads legend became popular with the story of the renowned, American blues singer Robert Leroy Johnson and another musical colleague, Tommy Johnson. Both say they met a mysterious helper at the crossroads. There are many versions of this tale—all with a variety of storytelling—but I'm going to choose the most popular version and tell the one about Robert Johnson, who recorded in the thirties. According to the legend, as a young man living on a plantation in rural Mississippi, Robert Johnson wanted to become a great blues musician. He was instructed to take his guitar to a crossroad at midnight. There he was met by a mysterious black man who took the guitar and tuned it up to perfection. The crossroads spirit played a few songs and then returned the guitar to Johnson, giving him mastery over the instrument. Robert Johnson was able to create great blues music and become famous for it. I have always loved that story. As a matter of fact, Robert Johnson's music in the background is helping me to write this chapter; that is inspiration at its best!

With further research and study, I have learned that the idea of a crossroads as a supernatural entryway is not uncommon. The crossroads is a place that is not claimed by the living or the dead; it's an in-between place where our physical world and the supernatural world merge. While investigating house hauntings, I have experienced several instances in which the origin of the supernatural happenings happened at the crossroads near those houses.

In this work, I'm going to describe my experiences, insight, and thoughts about the supernatural. I am on a symbolic journey and standing at the crossroads to record a very elusive reality that at one point or another will cross the threshold into our everyday existence. At that time, we will be forever changed in the way that we see life, death, and destiny. With each chapter, you will enter a different crossroads into other realms, deepening your understanding of what resides behind the inspirited curtain that separates us from the others. All of my books have been a journey and an evolution of my own spiritual viewpoints. This book is the most intimate of all because it is where I truly live and breathe. For the first time, I am opening up and exposing my innermost, cherished supernatural experiences. I'm sharing them with you as examples of a big, wide world that surrounds us but is not located within the physical. In an honest moment here, I admit that the supernatural world is where I am most comfortable. Whenever I pass a crossroads, I always feel comforted by the fact that no matter how concrete, plastic, or fake this world gets, there are still some actual supernatural wonders and magic somewhere in this great country of ours. No one can duplicate or fake the real supernatural. The answers are at the crossroads, and we are all headed there to see what wonders await.

The Veil: Pay Attention to the Man behind the Curtain

"Curiouser and curiouser!"
—Lewis Carroll, *Alice's Adventures in Wonderland*

Since the beginning of time, man has been fascinated and even obsessed with the unseen worlds that exist all around us. From the communion of spirits within sacred rituals performed by our ancestors to the saturation of current paranormal reality television, a deep desire to know and connect with the mystery behind the invisible curtain that separates our world from "theirs" is in our very core. I truly believe that even the harshest of skeptics embraces a quiet wonder of what else lies beyond in the unknown realms. I myself was born into a world of ghosts and folklore. In the Ozark Mountains of Arkansas there still lives a rich tradition of spiritualism and magic. Underneath the very buckle of the Bible belt, it is easy to sense that there is mystery and supernatural wonder in those hills. For whatever reason, souls that lost their way hundreds of years ago continue to wander in a perpetual dream state, lost in the dark forests of the Ozarks. I have felt them. I have heard the lonely cries calling from a world beyond mine.

As a child, the supernatural was natural to me. My grandmother filled my childhood with stories from her own childhood of things going bump in the night, ghosts walking up creaky stairs, and spiritual miracles of healing performed by granny witches who had the power of herb and chant. Little did I know at the time that my grandmother was telling me of very real occurrences. She was nurturing my own abilities to see these things for myself by keeping my mind open to the possibility of different realities. I realized long ago in metaphor that the "man behind the curtain" was real, and I should pay attention—*close attention.*

What if the dark figure we have seen in the corner of the room were real? Or what about the big, hairy creature that ran across the road one rainy night; was that Bigfoot? How would you see your life then? Accept that all of the ghost stories, angelic encounters, mystical visions, and the monsters of folklore just might be real. You might sense a completely new dimension of living if you allow yourself to believe, just for a moment, that the realms of the supernatural and its inhabitants are as real as the pages of this book. We can recognize that the interest in what is beyond the veil is at its peak these days just by watching the subject matter on films and TV and by reading about it in published media.

The reason I wanted to write this particular book and throw in my two cents' worth on the subject was to give you, the seeker, a more grounded and factual perspective on a very elusive reality. This book will help direct you with some discernment to the many mansions be-yond our world. With the sweet, comes the sour, and with the many op-portunities of publishing and video accessibility, anyone and everyone can throw out their thoughts on psychic and supernatural studies. Some of it's good, and some of it is just plain baloney. I could not stand by any longer without writing a book that would help the seeker take a more authentic look at these matters. I'm not saying I'm the final word when it comes to understanding and navigating the supernatural, but I do know enough from my own studies and my own personal experiences not to journey into the unknown without a life rope tied to a strong spiritual foundation. Again, with anything psychic or supernatural, there will always be room for growth and room for expanding one's mind. If you have a strong spiritual ideal that you live by, you can freely move and discover more psychic landscapes with safety and ease. This book will describe more about the supernatural landscape.

My books on building a strong spiritual foundation are revealed in *Reader of Hearts: The Life and Teachings of a Reluctant Psychic* and *Becoming Masters of Light: Co-Creating the New Age of Enlightenment.* I would strongly suggest reading my aforementioned works to prepare you for stepping into this highly intense realm of understanding.

I think that I am more excited about writing this book than any other. My life has been so absorbed with the supernatural that to finally write about my findings and experiences is truly important to me as a psychic investigator and researcher. In my previous book, *Becoming Masters of Light,* I came out of the closet for the second time, but as a practicing exorcist. This story gave my readers a small glimpse into my world as far as dealing with dimensions beyond what we see with the physical eye. Many of you who are reading this work have also seen a glimpse beyond the veil, or you would not have happened upon this book. This will not be a scientific work that tries to prove the reality of the supernatural. I have no interest in proving anything. I am a researcher, yes, and a psychic investigator, all the time, but I'm not a scientist. I'm simply interested in sharing my experience, my insights, and my views on a very challenging topic. Don't get me wrong, evidence that there is actually a man behind the curtain, per se, is extremely beneficial, and I love it when my colleagues discover this reality. Even though I'm interested to hear what's been found, I also know and don't hesitate to say, "See, I told you so."

Always remember that the veil between worlds is an intelligence all its own and will reveal itself along with its supernatural inhabitants when it wants to do so. I love the scientific folks, but some of them who think that they are scientific are laughable. I ran into a self-proclaimed "copy-and-paste" paranormal investigator (we will call him Barry), who was gung ho about proving his investigations with the paranormal. He had co-authored a few books with another self-proclaimed paranormal scientist, and together they were pretty funny. With all their "research" and video presentations, they seemed to focus more on proving their work with the paranormal rather than concentrating on the paranormal by itself. That's always a red flag for me, when I see ego first and actual, legitimate research later. There are many personalities of that type in this business. Misrepresentation makes it difficult for my friends and colleagues who are actually doing good field work to publish their information without slander or even theft. Consequently, you will see in my work a mere sharing of stories, and any research that I'm detailing will be credited wholeheartedly to the true person of origin.

The veil between the realms deserves respect and integrity. It is not something to be seen as a joyride at an amusement park. We are gradually opening up spiritually and psychically to the veil as an awareness of what's truly vibrating around us, and any investigation is for the purpose of knowledge and understanding. Remember that when we incarnated on this planet in this life and in other lives, we had to pass through the spectral membrane. At death, we will do it again. The veil is familiar with us and with all souls, so its discovery in our own lives is that of a deep and ancient remembrance. When you read these pages and ponder the stories and the information, remember that the supernatural is an ever-changing vibration of mystery and discovery. It is our one single question of "who is that man behind the curtain" that will truly reveal a world among worlds as well as our spiritual heritage and destiny.

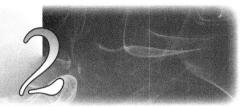

The Dark Realm

"If you place your head in a lion's mouth, then you cannot complain one day if he happens to bite it off."—Agatha Christie

We begin our journey into the many realms of the supernatural with the Dark Realm. This is a fascinating realm and one with which I'm very familiar. It may sound obscure and foreboding—true—but this realm is like the others, which are all part of God's many dimensions. With the sweet comes the sour, and with the rose comes the thorn. As a practicing exorcist and spiritual healer, I have had considerable edification and experience with the shadows that possess people, whether the shadows are self-induced or come from an outside force. Either way, this particular realm is very interesting. It is home not only to supernatural beings but also to our own reflections of the shadows and fears by which we might allow ourselves to be controlled. Negative projections, evil intent, glamour, illusion, and demonic intelligences are the inhabitants here. What's interesting about this realm is that it is the farthest away from the Creator. It's an area of rebellion. All beings that choose to turn away from the Divine Light of the Source realm make this their chaotic presence of residence.

The Divine Light represents truth, liberation, peace, awareness, justice, and all aspects of healing and balance. When I refer to light and dark, I'm not talking about a religious god vs. Satan, even though those are well-formed archetypal symbols. I will not use or accept the religious dogma projected by some of the fundamentalist Christian groups. We all have the great power to choose to be lighthearted or dark-hearted. There are even those that live in the gray area of supernatural and human alike. It's not good, it's not bad, and it's all within the power of choice. Like the yin and yang symbol, within the white side there is a dot of black, and within the black side there is a dot of white. If we look at this symbol as a 3-D image, like a sphere, we can begin to see life and creation as a holistic design rather than just black and white designs. There is a need for both love and fear within the universe, and we learn and grow from both. When it comes to our spiritual natures, we have the divine right to choose what's healthy and what's not. Many people who come to me for healing or for an exorcism ritual are able to release their fears and their control issues as they allow a higher vibration to be their guide. I never judge souls on what path they want to take—either way, as I will say repeatedly, all souls will return to the Creator, the Source, at some point. In my own personal belief system, evil is never the way to go. I have seen the results of its hold on a soul and it is not pretty! But, I also know that many people who have experienced possessions and delved into the black arts have evolved out of that darkness. They discover their own power and receive a wider perspective and a deeper view of their own place in the world. Healing can happen for anyone and anything.

In most of the other realms, the Creator has charged many spiritual beings to reign, but in the Dark Realm there is commonly utter chaos. If there is any ruling factor to this realm, it is the archetypal force we call Satan that permeates and saturates the realm. The Christian mythological story states that Satan, an archangel, was cast out of heaven for not being a team player. Hell—or in my terms, the Dark Realm—was created, and Satan and his legions were cast into it permanently. There are many new age dogmas that consider Satan to be a symbol of man's ego, or a lower form of consciousness that is selfish and has no desire for spiritual evolution. Lucifer (the shining one) became another name for Satan in Christian theology. According to Jewish studies, Lucifer was cast out of heaven for not bowing down to Adam, who had charge over the earth. In Judaism and Christianity, Satan is represented as a fallen angel, but in Islamic studies, the devil is a djinn (or spiritual creature) and not an angel.

In folk traditions from Europe, the devil was known as the Old One or Old Split-foot. This persona did not carry the same role that Satan portrayed in Christianity and Judaism. Instead, he was a trickster. The word *old* has long been related to the devil, originally in respect to his primeval character. In Old English, he was called *se ealda* ("the old one"). For centuries, English speakers have invented all sorts of fantastic euphemisms for the devil using the word *old*. Examples include *Old Nick*, *Old Teaser*, and *Old Thief*. Some of the devil's nicknames are based on the traditional representation of him with horns and cloven hooves, which were initiated by Christians in the Middle Ages. They pictured the devil as an evil figure modeled after the pagan deity, Pan, who was part human and part goat. Those characteristics led to the names *Old Hornie* and *Split-foot*. In my view, there is a trickster spirit and the spirit of truth, and we have the fun of choosing which one to work with.

This chapter deals with the realm of the darkness that can intervene in our lives and create havoc, but note that it's a two-way street. The Dark Realm can't come to play if you don't invite it. It's like meeting the devil at the crossroads: if you make a deal, your bill will eventually have to be settled, and you are going to wish that you had not sealed the pact. There is always a price to pay when working with the Dark Realm. It's a tricky area. This realm has its own agenda and intent that has nothing to do with your well-being or profit.

Vengeful Spirits

Let's talk about some of the beings that inhabit the Dark Realm. First on the tour are the vengeful spirits. Our friends at *Wikipedia* (last modified December 4, 2013), define a vengeful spirit like this: "In mythology, and folklore, a vengeful ghost or vengeful spirit is said to be the spirit of a deceased person who returns from the afterlife to seek revenge for a cruel, unnatural, or unjust death. In certain cultures where funerals and burial or cremation ceremonies are important, such vengeful spirits may also be considered as unhappy ghosts of individuals who have not been given a proper funerary rite." In my work, I have found this definition to be true. Souls that have had prolonged afterlives steeped in anger and resentment tend to become more and more concentrated in negativity. This form reaches far beyond a simple lost soul or a ghost who haunts an old farmhouse. These souls can become concentrated evil. Therefore they reside in the Dark Realm and not in the Paranormal Realm.

My first encounter with a vengeful spirit occurred when a client contacted me about a disturbance in his household. He and his wife were newly married and were living in a lovely cabin way out in the country. They literally lived a rural life on a small farm equipped with well water and no electricity, and yes, there was even an outhouse. There are many country people who call me when needed due to their trust and my reputation as a local from the Ozarks. No citified psychics for them!

The husband had been getting scratch marks on him from out of nowhere, and his clothing would be thrown all over the place when they returned from a trip to town. This occurrence happened on several occasions. The last straw happened when my client felt a blow to the head while he was in the kitchen and fell to the floor. No one else was there. His wife was visiting her sister that day in another town. As I drove about twenty miles out into the country on the dirt road, I could see the sun setting over the Ozarks. I had a feeling this was going to be an eventful night, so I had stocked up on holy water, sacred objects, and my special remedies for blessings and spiritual cleansings. I took along my friend Carol, who at that time had been working with me for about five years. We have been working together for twenty years now, so this particular encounter happened some time ago.

When we arrived, the couple was on the front porch, looking terrified.

"It's already started," he yelled as he walked quickly to the car with the young wife in tow.

I got out of the car and could feel an energy emanating from the house. It was a wall of tremendous anger. Something was not at all happy that I had shown up. I don't scare off easily; as a matter of fact, I don't scare off at all. So this energy was about to mess with the wrong psychic tonight! The challenge was on, so I prayed and invoked my spiritual protectors immediately. Carol usually went with me into the locations for blessings, but on this night, I knew that she was not strong enough to deal with this bad force.

I told the others to stay outdoors, and as I walked into the house, I noticed it was lit only with kerosene lamps. I normally like the smell of kerosene, as it reminds me of warmth on a winter's night. On this night, however, the lamps created a perfect setting for a supernatural happening as the shadows played back and forth on the cabin walls.

As I stepped across the threshold, a broom fell, or was thrown down, rather, right in front of me. I stepped over it and kept walking around the room. The living room was to my left, so I entered it and walked around, sending out my psychic feelers to locate the origin of the paranormal disturbance. I closed my eyes and took a deep breath. There he was. A lost soul who was seething with anger was standing just behind me. I could watch him trying to punch me within my mind's eyes. He was hitting and slapping, but I felt nothing.

"Sorry buddy, it won't work," I said. "Why don't you talk to me, and try to calm down."

A wedding picture that I was standing next to crashed to the floor. Then, I heard a crash from upstairs. I walked upstairs, still talking aloud to the angry specter. I walked into the young couple's bedroom and found what looked like a jewelry box that had crashed to the floor.

The shouting words of "NO! NO! NO! I hate them! I hate them!" kept ringing through my brain. I knew it would require more than just my usual ghost therapy session to take care of this business. I walked back outside. Everyone was standing around the car looking wide-eyed.

"What the hell is going on in there?" Carol asked. I could tell she was in full attack mode.

"Okay, kids, we have a vengeful spirit to deal with. Fasten your seat belts; it's going to be a bumpy night!" (Yeah, I pulled my inner Bette Davis big-shouldered broad out for effect.)

I instructed the ensemble to sit in a circle in the middle of the living room. I had Carol cover all the mirrors in the room; nasty spirits have been known to use them as portals of escape. I surrounded our circle with salt—but only partly, like a crescent moon. I wanted to allow space for the spirit to enter our circle and communicate. As you will learn later in this book, ghosts cannot cross a line of salt. Salt is a spiritual protectant. I placed a white candle in the middle of the circle, and we all sat down in chairs.

Let me mention at this time that spirit contact is a very tricky situation if you do not know what you are doing. *Do not try this at home.* Unless you have been taught respectful mediumship and know all the tricks of the trade, stay far away from situations like this one. I knew that this case was going to require mediumship as well as casting a circle of power to contact this spirit and draw him in. He was a vengeful spirit, and a house blessing would only fix the problem temporarily. Unlike the presence of a demonic being where I could call forth the Archangel Michael and have it bound, this spirit might be treated the same, but I wanted to make sure to give him a chance to heal his vengefulness. I don't give demons the time of day—they have to go!

Usually it's best to have others of psychic and mediumship training in your spirit circles, but this occasion was a situation of extreme measures. I needed the spiritual intent and power of the couple to help with the process of contact. It was also Carol's first time, but I knew she was ready to put her training into action if she had to.

There was only the soft glow of the candle and the kerosene lamps in the room. As we sat down, I began to instruct those in the circle about their jobs. Carol was to keep the prayer book handy in case the spirit became more agitated than normal. The couple was to answer any questions they might have concerning the spirit once he was contacted.

Vengeful spirits may be very unpredictable, just like any energy from the Dark Realm. Their means are to punish and hurt, and in certain cases, it is for correct justice. Nevertheless, it's best to communicate with respect and with a sense of authority, and whenever possible, it is preferable to treat the cause and send them on their way to the light. Spirit contact in this case is for the purpose of healing on both sides of the veil.

This night was not about a slumber party or a realty show, so there was no disrespect in our space. I began to relax and call for my spiritual power and guardians for protection. I invoked a member of the legion of the Archangel Michael to be with us and be on guard in case we needed him. As soon as I gave the signal, Carol's job was to close the circle with salt immediately after the spirit had entered it. Closing the circle traps the spirit so that we can get the job done.

I began to use my own method of trance and started the process of invoking the vengeful spirit. I'm not going to give you my formula, and I don't want anyone to do this practice at home—opening up Pandora's Box. As I began to breathe deeply, the crashing of pans in the kitchen made the members of the circle jump. Carol, right on cue, kept the prayers going and the intention strong. As the spirit moved closer to the circle, we could feel the temperature drop in the room. Suddenly, a chilly breeze encircled everyone, and I gave the nod for Carol to close the circle. She did, and we had him.

As some of you know from my last work, I don't encourage mediumship or spirit contact. Let me clarify this statement. Picture an ordinary man walking into a mental hospital and trying to diagnose and treat mental cases. It's the same thing in this situation. If you are trained, well versed in the supernatural, and have a high psychic clarity of discernment, then you can work this kind of ritual, but in most cases it is not advisable. Most people see mediumship and spirit contact butchered and commercialized on television shows, and there is no respect as a result. If you don't have any respect for the spirit world and the supernatural, you are going to be burned.

When I go into trance, it's as though my consciousness of Darrin sits off in a corner of my mind and watches everything that's happening. I told the Creator that if I were to do this work, I wanted to be conscious of everything. I did not want any part of blacking out or not remembering who started chatting through my vocal cords. I also chose to relay the messages I receive from a spirit without having my body taken over by that spirit. Yeah, I have my boundaries, even with the spirits!

I began to feel myself go under, and I stepped through the veil into the realm in which this vengeful spirit was residing. It was dark, it was creepy, and he was *very* angry! In my mind, I saw the two of us in a room. It was the living room where the circle was gathered, but only he and I were present. The spirit was a young man in his early twenties. He wore jeans and a red and black checkered shirt.

"Why are you here?" The spirit shouted. (I made sure to vocalize everything for the team on the other side.)

"I'm here to help you," I said calmly.

"He took her from me!"

"Who?" I said.

"Roger, the (bleep) son of a (bleep) took her away. I want him dead. I want him dead!" (Roger was my client.)

"First of all, who are you?" I asked. Still calm.

"Bobbie, my name is Bobbie, and why am I here?" He began to cry uncontrollably.

When I repeated the name Bobbie, I could hear the couple gasp from the other side.

"I trusted him, and he took her away from me."

"Okay, let's talk about you," I said. "What happened; do you remember anything? What's the last thing you remember?"

The first thing to do with any lost souls is to try to bring back some awareness by pulling them out of their fog. Bobbie stopped crying and became very still, just staring into the darkness.

"I remember a loud noise; it hurt my ear." Bobbie pointed to the right side of his head.

He turned to look at me, and suddenly I began to feel the right side of my face become numb. Carol reported later from the other side that my face actually looked as if I had had a stroke. My face began to droop, and even though it freaked her out, she knew to keep the energy moving without doing anything until I gave a signal.

From the other side of the veil, I could feel my head pounding and I could not talk.

I saw Bobbie coming closer and closer to me, and he started trying to take me over. *Hell, no!* The vengeful spirit was trying to merge with my energy. I managed to give a finger signal, and Carol began a prayer of protection and exorcism. Bobbie was not going to cooperate, and within the darkness of the other side, I saw a wolf jumping from that darkness toward Bobbie. The spirit freaked and fell to his knees. The wolf stood between the spirit and me. This was an odd occurrence even for me, but it was all happening.

The wolf turned to me as if to say, "Go back to the other side; I got this."

Then, immediately, I popped out of the trance in a cold sweat. I opened my eyes to a very blurry vision of the couple holding each other and crying. Carol was frozen, still repeating the prayer.

"Okay, okay," I said, "enough of the dramatics. It's all good." I stood up and went outside, or I tried to. I was wiped. I motioned for the gang to follow me, and I sat on the steps of the porch. I pulled out a cigarette and lit it. Don't judge me here, dear reader; they are organic, and I enjoy smoking.

"Okay, kids," I said. "So Bobbie shoots himself and has a vendetta against you, Roger. And you, the little woman, used to be Bobbie's girlfriend."

All were in agreement, and the entire story came out. Roger and

Bobbie had been childhood pals. The previous year after breaking up with his girlfriend, Bobbie, who had some significant emotional problems, killed himself. He shot himself on the right side of the head. Sadly, it did not kill him. He was still conscious. He tried to walk out of the house but unfortunately tripped and fell down the ravine behind his home into the creek below. He died face down in the water—a very tragic death. A few months afterward, Roger and Bobbie's girlfriend began a strong friendship, which later turned into marriage. It was not long after their wedding that the couple moved into their own cabin, which was a few miles away from where the tragedy had happened. They began to notice a few incidents like cold spots and the oil lamps dimming more than usual. It was not until a few of their friends came over for a Halloween party that things grew a bit more active. A guest brought over a spirit board. Messing with a spirit board will manifest two actions, spirit contact and spirit release. The damned boards are so unpredictable that I tell folks to burn them. Unfortunately for the couple, a spirit release occurred. The board opened the door between realms even wider to permit Bobbie's enraged soul to come through and wreak his vengeance.

After hearing the story, of course I scolded the couple and reminded them that this entire night was about having respect for the dead and not "playing in the fields of the Lord" when you don't know the rules. When I told them about the wolf appearing, Roger was amazed. He clarified that once when they were kids playing in the woods, a wolf had appeared and chased them. They were not harmed as they made it back to their own property and safely into Bobbie's home, but it freaked the kid out. Bobbie never really conquered his fear of wolves or even dogs. I knew in my heart that a protector and guardian manifested as a wolf in order to restrain Bobbie's spirit. The spiritual support that we have within our grasp is incredible. The guardian relayed that Bobbie's spirit was bound and taken to a place called "sanctuary" in the spirit realm. You will learn about this particular subject later in the book.

After I recovered my wits and found my footing, I re-entered to check the house thoroughly. It was free and clear. The couple has never had a problem since that night. With any soul that I'm trying to help, at times there is success, and at other times, the situation has to be surrendered to the Creator. Some spirits choose to remain in their chaos and misery.

No matter what, they will always be given a chance to recover and heal in the fullness of time.

Demonic Spirits and Dark Souls

Demonic spirits are another ball game compared to vengeful spirits. Demonic spirits are concentrated evil, void of all awareness of light or the Creator's grace. Dark souls are human spirits that have become demonized. A human soul can mutate close to a demonic spirit if it chooses to do so. Serial killers and souls that have lived very evil lives can leave their bodies and become demonic. Demons are spirits that have been around since the early days of creation. Through the years, many stories have filtered through civilizations about just exactly what a demon is. Some scholars state that demons are Satan's angels who left heaven with him to become a legion of chaos and tempters. With the purpose to drive a wedge between God and man, they are a legion of rebellion. They are considered to be fallen angels, unclean spirits, or lesser gods, although the word demon currently connotes an attachment to evil. Originally, it was a neutral term for any spirit who ranked below a deity.

Demons have opposed a number of significant spiritual masters from world religions such as the Hindu gods, Buddha, Jesus, and even the Source—the Creator. It is believed universally that only faith in divine love can overcome these creatures. I have found that belief to be true in my own work with exorcism and banishing rituals. These energies, although powerful with their own psychic powers of manipulation, can be overcome by faith in your own spiritual power as a child of God. The demonic forces want you to forget that belief. The dark souls have been corrupted by demons. After death, depending on the soul and its free will, this corrupted soul may be taken even further into the Dark Realm. Vengeful spirits are at great risk for this journey into more dark-ness. That's why I had to do everything possible to encourage Bobbie to enter the light of the spirit world. Demons can only travel within the Dark Realm, the Nature Realm, and the Paranormal Realm. Currently, we investigators are finding demonic types of entities of a new breed, or at least to new to us, in the Multidimensional Realm. We call them the djinn creatures. I have decided to explain the djinn in the Multidimensional Realm chapter due to their unique nature of not following the usual demonic modus operandi.

There is always something to discover in the supernatural realms. Demons are also regarded as images for natural disasters, illness, and viciousness—related to the "deadly sins" in Christian theology. Demons are also used to describe the shadow self of our inner fears and anxieties: hence the expression: "face your inner demons." Encounters with demons can be frightening, as they seem to be a spiritual threat. At times, demons pose a physical threat by possessing humans and driving them mad. They plant fear within the mind and heart of the victim to black out the light of the Creator in someone's soul. I know that I'm writing about some "heavy stuff" here, but this is a very serious and important subject. I want to inform and educate my readers. Again, this book presents my own research, experience, and perception. Please use your intuition about anything you read to see if it fits for you.

Over the centuries and with the widespread growth of Christianity, demons began to represent all sorts of things. Pagan gods were misconstrued as demons, and fairy folks and inhabitants of the Nature Realm became demonized, also. People who had special gifts or were blessed with the magical arts of nature were demon-possessed. The very ideas that demons love are confusion, misguided truths, and injustice for innocent beings. We can see the demonic influence in history in situations like the Salem witch trials. The demonic force was not in the people accused of witchcraft but in the accusers who stood in the pulpit and lit the fires to burn the supposed witches. Things have not changed much today.

Humans can be quite stupid, arrogant, and ego-driven, creating the right environment for a demon to blink an eye and catch another idiot's attention. Most people can be turned without even knowing it. That's why spiritual empowerment is so important. When you're connecting to the Source, the Creator cannot be shaken. So, regardless of the origin of demons, devils, or any dark archetypal forces, remember that they are real—and bad—and not to be messed with! These energies haunt our outside world via the supernatural. In addition, we often create our own shadow demons with our negative projections and intentions. In my other works, I explain many ways to stabilize and balance your inner self spiritually in order to keep the shadow self in control.

The Energetics of Possession and Spirit Attachment

As a practicing exorcist, I have had the great privilege of researching in detail the spiritual or energy mechanics, if you will, of what we know of as spirit possession. The entities of the Dark Realm are very parasitic in nature as they seek any way to step through the veil to attach to the living and use their life force as a drug to experience, manipulate, and cause havoc. We, the human souls within our physical realm, can be affected by these energies. Think of it this way, when you go walking through a dense part of the woods without a bug repellent, you will in fact invite little critters like ticks and chiggers to attach themselves to your ankles. This is the same process for the supernatural, except instead of using bug repellent, you protect your life with spiritual power and awareness.

As we know, everything is energy. Thanks to Einstein, we know that energy cannot be created or destroyed, but it can be transformed. That idea is the foundation of my work with exorcism. Exorcism is an essential aspect to my work as a psychic and spiritual healer. Spiritual deliverance—or exorcism—is a powerful healing agent for every soul on this planet. Learning to abolish fear and embrace love is the ultimate salvation for humankind. Understanding the energetics of the process of possession will help you to maintain your supernatural awareness while keeping your auric field intact. In my book, *Becoming Masters of Light*, I wrote extensively about how someone might attract negative vibrations. Possession always begins with a choice. You can choose to invite the dark forces into your life, or you can choose to sweep them out of your life. It's important to be vigilant with your own personal power and consciousness.

Spirit Attachment and Demonic Possession

My work in this area began when I was in my early twenties. When most "baby" psychics were learning to "read auras and tarot cards," I was learning the tricks of the trade in de-possession and spirit-release therapy. As my mentors have always said, spiritual deliverance work is where the real healing happens. Whether one is exorcising negative thoughts by prayer or whether an exorcist is performing a complete deliverance, the healing power of the Creator is working to balance and restore divine love to right all wrongs. That's the foundation of healing.

It can be very frightening to think that some kind of alien force could seep its way into our spiritual bodies. To suddenly be controlled by a phantom intelligence makes for captivating supernatural thrillers. Believe it or not, there are a few grains of truth in the Hollywood fictional movies. Throughout history, the reality of possession has filtered through the lives of countless souls from every background and religion. The most recognizable on the subject of exorcism is the New Testament in the Holy Bible. The focus that was always associated with the Master Jesus was that his healing ministry went hand in hand with exorcism.

> *And Jesus stepped ashore; a certain man from the town met him who was possessed by demons. For a long time this man had worn no clothes and had not lived in a house, but among the tombs. Jesus started commanding the evil spirit to come out of the man. The evil spirit seized the man many times so he would be bound with chains and shackles and kept under guard. The people went out to see what had happened and they came to Jesus. They found the man, from whom the demons had gone out, sitting at Jesus' feet, clothed and in his right mind. Those who had seen it told them how the man who had been demon possessed had been healed.*
> (The Holy Bible, Luke 8:27-36.
> [New English Translation])

The beautiful metaphysics of this story of the master exorcist Jesus Christ using spiritual deliverance as a healing agent is a prime example of the true meaning and focus of exorcism. Christianity, depending on the denomination, still recognizes exorcism as a legitimate practice in spiritual healing. There are others such as Voodoo, Hoodoo, and Native American practices. I would like to disregard the religious fanatical perspective in order to look at possession and exorcism for the true, essential supernatural reality that it is. Some use this process as a brainwashing technique to hold people in fear, but the aforementioned Bible story clearly demonstrates that a soul can be released from the negative shackles and chains of an unsound mind. We cloud our minds when we live with anger, hate, and depression as our primary emotions. I think that one of the main reasons people become possessed or find themselves engaged in negative paranormal activity is an unabashed disrespect for the workings of the supernatural. Playing with fire will get you burned! If you have no respect for the supernatural, you have no business playing in the fields of the Lord, as I always say.

The Possession of the Energy Anatomy

As some of you may already know or have read in my earlier books, there is a spiritual anatomy or an energy anatomy that vibrates within us. Just as we have a physical body, we also have an energy body. The energy body is what is affected when it comes to spiritual attachments or full-blown demonic possession. Our spiritual energy body vibrates an energy that surrounds our body, which is called the aura. The human aura is a field of subtle, luminous emission that surrounds us and extends outward from our physical form.

Auras are related to the electromagnetic field of the body and serve as a visual measure of our mental, emotional, physical, and spiritual

states. When I'm working with clients and sense their auric energy, there are times when I can detect like radar an alien energy hovering near or even rooted in their aura. Dark murky-colored orbs or splotches may show up. At times, a pure, concentrated blackness like the silhouette of a human form may be present in the aura. Think of it this way: the attachment of a spirit is like finding a spider crawling on your leg while possession is like discovering the spider bites on that leg.

Most of the time, our energy anatomy and its auric field are rotating all the colors of the rainbow, depending on our emotional and mental states. Also, if we are fueling our own negativity, the bright rainbow colors may become faded and dark. When our aura is affected by our own self-induced emotions, the energy still looks like part of a painting. When the aura is affected by an outside source, something does not look right; there is a part of the painting that should not be there. The energy feels dislocated and has a mind of its own.

In spirit attachments, a soul that is lost attaches to the outside of a person's living aura and it hovers. It wants to hang out with the person like a fly that won't go away. The soul that has not yet found its way through the light to the Spiritual Realm continues to desire life on this physical plane. So, it begins to live your life with you! Unfortunately, the longer the soul attaches to your energy, the more it can drain away your life force. You, the living victim, may exhibit great fatigue, physical ailments that have no reason to be present, and confusion or emotional states and thoughts that are not yours. Spirit attachments usually begin at the upper part of the aura near the head and shoulders. The closer the earthbound attachment becomes and the deeper it's allowed to invade, the more the victim becomes like that outside intelligence. Spirit attachment does not always occur on purpose.

Through loneliness, addiction, fear, or even a displaced love, a spirit might attach to a living person. It desires the feeling of life and a chance to live once again in the physical realms. Sometimes by mistake, the spirit entity attaches to a living person it has been hanging around and will not realize that it is affecting the victim adversely. Demonic possession, on the other hand, occurs absolutely on purpose with the intent to disempower the victim and crush his or her soul. Demonic possession starts at the very bottom of the auric field, seeping its way into the root chakra area of a human being. It's like pure, concentrated blackness or even a deep, dark red energy that worms its way up the energy anatomy until it has possessed the entire being.

The demonic spirit "wants in"—it wants to be inside the mental, emotional, and physical body until it is able to overcome the spiritual body—and then it devours the victim until there is nothing left. In dealing with demonic spirits, it's best to contact a trained exorcist, conjure doctor, or shaman who is trained in these matters. Do not ever challenge a demon! Below are a few signs of demonic interference and invasion.

Demons may appear with a few physical signs of their presence:

- The odor of sulfur or rotted meat.
- Scratching sounds on the walls of a location.
- Paranormal disturbances occurring between 3:00 to 3:45 a.m. This is the most powerful time for any supernatural occurrence to take place. Demons take advantage of that power. Some call this period "dead time."
- Appearances of shadow figures or dark, hooded figures. Current research, however, may reveal that these figures are actually djinn manifestations.
- The destruction of sacred objects. I've seen all types of sacred objects from a variety of religious practices be tossed like a Frisbee across a room. It's not just the Christians that the demons mess with.
- Feelings of impending doom, death, or insanity from an unknown source may also surface.
- Immediate changes of attitude, such as hatred, vengeance, and murderous tendencies may develop.
- Physical harm to a victim may occur once possession has taken hold.

Please don't become upset or start freaking out here, dear reader. It is important to know that demonic possession and attack are not as prevalent as Hollywood portrays or as some might think. Most demons don't bother with the usual "exorcist" routine anymore. These days, demons want to influence the most gullible people to wreak havoc, just as religious fundamentalists, cult leaders, and politicos might do.

Please note that demons can be invoked in the same manner as the angelic powers. If you use your powers of invocation to summon forth demons to do your bidding, be ready to pay the piper, and be ready for the chance to have your head bitten off, too!

Demons always start their campaigns of possessing a human with the use of mental and emotional manipulation. Depending on the person, they may begin to insert thoughts of powerfulness, egotism, and self-inflation. A soul who has weakened its energy because of envy and a lust for power provides an open door for a demon to strike a deal with that soul. Also, demons go after those who are very psychic and spiritually attuned. They do not want any more souls with the gifts of the spirit to be walking the planet, so they try to infuse them with feelings of loneliness, despair, and even suicide. I now realize that my bout with strong feelings of separation and suicide when I was fifteen years old did not happen solely because people did not understand me; it was demonic attack. I suppose the demons felt threatened that I might become more aware of who I was. With the blessings and protection of my spiritual ancestors and the Holy Spirit, I won, and I learned early on that I had the gift of exorcism.

I will list a few more books at the end of this work for you to research on your own to deal with the demonic forces. I don't like to give them attention if I can help it, other than to educate people about their reality. Let me remind you that keeping your spiritual light bright is the only way to ward off these negative energies. Working on your thought power—staying strong like a steel trap—is also an essential practice. I'll provide some powerful prayers at this end of this book to help you.

Moving along, de-possession of a spirit attachment is much easier. It's a type of ghost therapy. These days, when clients come to me with spirits attached to their auras, I spend a moment of communication with these lost souls and can usually move them over to the Spiritual Realm very quickly. In the old days, many others and I used hypnosis. By deep trance hypnosis, the therapist uses the client to channel the attached spirit. This process allows the hypnotist to speak with the spirit *through* the hypnotized client. Another method is the use of a psychic medium to channel the attached spirits. The trained medium identifies attached spirits and entities and allows them to speak through him or her. Over time, I found that these methods took far too long, so I began communicating with the souls myself. I used my own formula for getting them to cross over. As I worked with the guardians of the other side and gained increasingly more hands-on experience in this work, I composed an invocation that does the job thoroughly. The invocation eases the process of helping spirits to cross over or be exorcised from a living individual. The spirit release technique through a hypnosis process is a great way to help lost souls if one is not gifted with psychic mediumship or the ability to pierce the veil.

In conclusion, the Dark Realm contains beings of shadow, mystery, and illusory intentions. Even though it's an essential part to the supernatural world, it is certainly a realm in which we must tread lightly. Remember that power invoked from the Dark Realm has a price, and it's never a good one. The only power worth discovering is your own spiritual power of magic, creation, and valour.

The Nature Realm

A s you walk into a thicketed forest, you can smell the evergreen foliage with its sweet, woodsy fragrance. You might feel the wind blow past as it takes a journey through the trees to parts unknown. The stillness of nature calls you to travel deeper and deeper into its realm. You realize at this time that you are hypnotized by the earth's intelligence and wisdom and that the wind is actually guiding you to the core of nature's beating heart. That core is like a distant drum, forever vibrating the song of God's creation. I am amazingly in love and completely devoted to the power of the Nature Realm in all her glory. I say "her" because we are going to delve into the kingdom of Gaia, which is Mother Earth.

I'm blessed enough to have returned to live near my childhood home in the Ozark Mountains, a place where nature still reigns. After living in concrete jungles like San Francisco and Los Angeles off and on for some years, I was schooled in the horrific damage that overcrowding, noise pollution, and the distancing from nature can do to one's soul. For several months, I worked on a few television and theater projects. I also taught intuitive acting classes in Los Angeles. I lived near Wilshire Boulevard, and there was not a moment's peace during any day or night. I would try to sleep among the sounds of cars honking, police and ambulance sirens, screaming people, and even gunshots. Not only was I on constant guard, but I also realized that I had nowhere to go to connect with nature or to feel any peace. All the beaches and parks were full of people, and unless you were a millionaire or a movie star, you did not have access to any private gardens or beaches. In the mountains of Arkansas, I had grown up listening to the crickets sing me to sleep, and the only ruckus of any kind came from the rooster when the sun rose in the morning. Even then, he became quiet after he felt that his duty was done. While still living, or trying to mentally survive in L.A., a realization struck me one day when I was lucky enough to visit my friend, singer and fellow spiritual healer Helen Reddy. She was staying with her son near Marina del Rey. After a long-needed chat and some tea, I was able to sit on the balcony of the condominium, overlooking the ocean.

Helen needed to get ready for an appearance that evening, so I had about an hour of *me* time. I sat quietly, looking into the ocean with its swells of tide coming in and going out, and it was like a practice of deep breathing. I realized I was breathing in harmony with the waves. I kept up the pace and began to feel the stress and anxiety of the city literally wash away with the tide as I inhaled and exhaled deeply. I was reconnecting with the earth. I was connecting to my grounding source, the source of all life, the Nature Realm. I felt peaceful and relaxed after so many months of energetic chaos. Over time, I realized that for the survival of my sanity and my spiritual work, I needed to return to nature and to a sense of peacefulness every day. I left the big-city life and found my way home, back to the Ozark Mountains of Arkansas. We still have seasons in this place, and there is a sense of pride in our culture. The Ozark Mountains surround our little town with protection and majesty. I have returned to sleeping peacefully to the singing of the crickets. I'm reminded of what Dorothy said in *The Wonderful Wizard of Oz*, "If I ever go looking for my heart's desire again, I won't look any further than my own back yard." Amen to that, girlfriend!

The Faery Folk: Guardian Angels of the Nature Realm

Believe it or not, the legends and tales of faery folk, elves, and gnomes are steeped in truth. These beings are not as much like Tinker Bell or the elves from Middle-earth as they are like light beings comprised of energy and intelligence. At times, these beings can and will appear in a physical form, but only to certain people. Sorry, folks, but this is not a chapter about how to talk to faeries. As a matter of fact, in my work and research, it seems that the faeries are not interested in human interaction. They would prefer for humans to leave them and the precious ecosystem alone. The Nature Realm has had a sour taste for us for many years since humans have not properly cared for our planet's environmental well-being. Throughout the years, the supernatural communities of the Nature Realm have tried desperately to educate us on ecology and the natural processes of Gaia, especially through the Findhorn Foundation and channeled material. Most recently, faery folk have become a new age, pop-culture gimmick. Tarot decks, books, classes, and how-to videos have swept the market regarding the Nature Realm's little residences. In my humble opinion, most of this material is not worth the expensive glossy paper on which it's printed. The tiny but powerful guardians of the Nature Realm have only one thing they hold most dear, and that is saving the planet from us. There are a few—and I emphasize a *few*—folks I have met that can sense the Nature Realm. Respect is the first and foremost ideal they ask of us. It is important to understand that these nature beings live and vibrate on a different level than we do, and they have a mission and purpose that God has charged them with: to create, protect, and nurture nature. Unfortunately, most of what they see is our disrespect for Gaia and her children, and that attitude can trigger them to project their energy onto unlucky persons who are hurting any animal or environmental area.

The faery folk are children of Mother Earth, so they can and will be as volatile as nature herself can be. I once had a client who was having terrible back pains, and he also had what looked like tiny bite marks up and down his legs. Doctors could not figure out what was going on and could not find anything to relieve the mysterious ailment. When the client sat down in my chair, I sensed he was a hunter. I could smell the blood of countless deer and other creatures in his energy. As we talked, he disclosed that he killed only for sport and sold skins for profit. He was a wealthy man and had no need to kill for food or clothing. It was solely for money. He casually mentioned this fact after I shared my insight of his being a hunter. I also had a vision of him shooting birds and squirrels, just because he could. His reply was that he got bored in the deer stand and needed something to do. I could feel my blood boil, and just as I was about to throw a punch at this jerk, I noticed a very tiny figure of light peeking behind the chair that he was sitting in.

As soon as I saw the little specter of a critter, I knew it was a nature being. I began to convey to the foolish client exactly what was causing his back pains and bite marks.

"You are being attacked by a faery. And with good reason," I replied.

The client looked at me and started laughing. Immediately as he started laughing, a welt appeared on his face, right before my eyes! The little nature being was not standing for any of this man's nonsense; he wanted justice, and he wanted to communicate to this fellow that he should never return to that part of the woods again because of his murderous tendencies. I relayed this information to the client. Meanwhile, he began to panic at the welt, which had grown to the size of a silver dollar. He promised he would stop. I further warned that there would be other nature spirits waiting for him if he went to another part of the woods. Then, I assured the little being that the man had received the message loudly and clearly. The little being bowed to me and was gone in the blink of an eye. Within a few minutes, the welt disappeared, and the client's back problems as well as the bites began to subside. To this day, that man has never hunted again.

In the old days, hunting was a necessity for survival, and there was an understanding between humans and the natural environment. The natural life cycle and ecological balance are respected on both sides of the veil. With respect and a reverence for the holiness of all life, Native Americans prayed and communed with the natural energies before every hunt. They knew that nature was not something to be conquered (as the pale faces thought). There are still certain people who think they are the "hunter of all hunters" and trample on the energetic landscapes of the Nature Realm, disturbing her peace and balance. They will receive what's coming to them.

I told the preceding story once in a workshop and was asked about communicating with the nature spirit. Did I have to exorcise it? Was it friendly? First of all, no. There was nothing to exorcise. This little critter was not an alien force invading the auric field of an individual. The faery was making a point and was bringing justice to his realm. It had every right to fight back and stop the invasion of his territory. God wants us to fight back when necessary, and that means all of his creations. The faery folk navigate the middle of the way between living and fear. Depending on the kind of faery folk and what they are guarding will point to what type of mood they will display. I want to point out that some excellent information about the faery folk I refer to can be found in the works of Orion Foxwood. Orion's mission with *The Faery Teachings* is for humans to reestablish a co-creative relationship with the natural realm. I agree completely. It is specifically our part in the separation between nature and ourselves that has caused such a wide rift. Our pollution, abuse, and destruction of animals and Mother Earth have done more damage than we can see with our physical eyes.

The Devas: Supreme Guardians of the Nature Realm

The devas are the supreme guardians of the Nature Realm. The faery folks take their direction from the devas, which are the spiritual intelligences behind nature. The origin of word "deva" comes from the Sanskrit language. There are numerous varieties of devas performing different functions on earth to help the Nature Realm function better. It is rare to actually see devas, as they like to hide behind the veil whenever possible. Those with psychic sight may see them from time to time.

I was lucky enough to see these beings a few times in my life. Once when I was a teenager, I took a walk deep into the woods. It was dusk and the sun was setting. I was working my way back to the dirt road that led back home when I spotted to my left a very tall, golden light hovering a few inches off the ground. Surrounding it were very tiny lights. It was a pleasant experience, but I also knew not to move close to it. It was gone just as quickly as it appeared. Later in life and after much research, I realized that I had seen a deva, and surrounding it had been the faery folk. I observed another being like it while backpacking in Sedona. My friend and I were hiking through Oak Creek Canyon when once again I stumbled onto a deva. My friend felt an intense energy, but I saw the tall, golden being manifest.

I nodded and it faded away. Suddenly the wind whipped up and whirls of air danced all around us; then, there was peace. The wind stopped. We kept hiking, and in my mind, I knew that I had encountered a deva of the air. There are countless devas and faery folks for every plant, animal, and mineral. Everything has a guardian on this planet. For example, if you are having problems growing tomatoes in your garden, even though you have a much-admired green thumb, ask the deva of tomatoes to help you. This deference is one component of the beginning of co-creation with the Nature Realm.

The Nature Realm will respond better to you if you ask respectfully and with a reverential petition. One summer, my kitchen was overrun with ants. The little buggers were in everything. Instead of buying poison and spraying them to death, I respectfully asked the deva of ants to please clear them out of my kitchen. To accompany my petition, I went into my back yard with an offering of natural sugar. I made a nice mound of it for the ants as my acknowledgment of appreciation. I have never had another ant problem again.

If you work with nature, nature will work with you. I'm often asked if humans can travel to the Nature Realm. As you have read, there are times when the veil thins, and we can take a peek into the faery world, but those are rare occurrences. If you are not fully in accord with the laws and support of Gaia, Mother Earth will not let you anywhere near her realm or her children. Our fur people, the animals and our pets, also have devas to guard them. Dogs, cats, and even creepy crawly creatures all are governed by their own specific devas. It's truly amazing how congruent and well-ordered the supernatural realms are. All of God's creations and mysteries are enveloped in his grace.

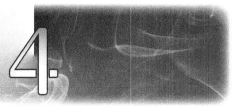

The Multidimensional Realm

"The Old Ones were, the Old Ones are, and the Old Ones shall be. Not in the spaces we know, but between them. They walk serene and primal, undimensioned and to us unseen."
—H.P. Lovecraft, *The Dunwich Horror and Others*

You know that drawer in your kitchen, the "anything" drawer where so many miscellaneous items end up? Those are assuredly important odds and ends, but they just don't fit anywhere else, so you toss them into the "anything" drawer for safekeeping. That description fits this chapter. Bigfoot, the Loch Ness Monster, aliens, UFOs, and other "cryptic creatures" will find their home here. Almost everything about supernatural wonders interests me, and the world of cryptozoology is important. We should not be so egotistical to believe that we are the only living creatures on this planet in addition to the animal and insect worlds. Nor should we believe that we are the only intelligence in the universe, but there will be more on that later. Some of these creatures seem to be here on earth, but not of the earth. They freely walk in and out of the veil as if it were a revolving door. Who are they? Where do they come from and what are their intentions? This is our current course, so let's get started.

Bigfoot

Some years ago, my assistant Carol and I were on our way to one of my healing events in southern Louisiana. We decided to leave a few days early because there was an interesting hot spot of investigation in Fouke, Arkansas. Fouke was on the way to my destination, and I had wanted to do a bit of detective work in the little town for years. The reason that this little town has such a big reputation is the fact that the area is reported to be the home of a Bigfoot creature, or the Southern Sasquatch, as it is called by outsiders. For over forty years, the creature has been sighted almost daily near the town of Fouke. During the early seventies, "The Fouke Monster" was accused of attacking a local family.

The monster was also blamed for the destruction of local livestock. Reports between 1971 and 1974 described the creature as being large and humanlike, covered in long, dark hair. It was estimated to be about seven feet tall, with a weight of 250–300 pounds. The locals said that its chest was about three feet wide. Later reports, published during the early eighties, claimed that it was far larger, with one report describing it as ten feet tall and weighing approximately 800 pounds. Either way, this creature is huge. In my own investigation, local people who have had firsthand experience with the creature described the Fouke Monster as running swiftly, even galloping, and swinging its arms like a monkey. Reports also describe it as having a terrible smell, like that of a skunk or a wet dog, with eyes that are large and bright red.

When we arrived in Fouke, there was a café and a gas station. That was pretty much the extent of the little town. If you blinked your eyes while driving down the road, you would literally pass by the town without even seeing it. We stopped in for a bite to eat at the café, and it must have been the lunchtime rush because all three parking spaces were taken. I'm from a small town and still live in a small town, so I had a good feeling that the locals would not mind chatting with me about their mysterious, furry resident. The waitress came over to our table as we sat down, and I was grateful that she poured coffee for me without even asking.

The waitress was my new best friend! She resembled the character Flo from the TV show Alice from the seventies. "Y'all are from out of town," she said, smacking her gum.

"Yes," I replied, "Little Rock." At the time, I resided in the "big-little" city.

"Oh, you're probably having culture shock way down here, sugar. What can I get ya?"

After we ordered up some good old-fashioned fried eggs, grits, bacon, and toast, I offhandedly mentioned wanting to talk to a few locals about the Fouke Monster.

"Oh, honey, you take your pick of anyone in here, even myself, and we have all seen him. You ain't with one of them snooty reality shows are ya?" Her face looked like she might pour some more coffee—but not into my cup!

"No ma'am; I'm just an Arkansas local interested in Arkansas stories." Since I had a bit of an accent, she accepted me. I was cleared for landing.

"Hey, fellas, this here boy wants to talk about the monster. You treat him nice now, he's okay."

The waitress must have been the watchdog, because after she gave me the green light, I was lucky enough to hear two hours' worth of stories from the five or six people who were in the restaurant. The waitress also talked to me when she took a cigarette break. The locals shared stories of hunting trips that went sour due to seeing the creature, who also scared the coon hounds. One hunter had been alone in the woods, just sitting there, when out from behind the tree stood the creature. It stared straight at him. The hunter did not move an inch and was terrified. Seeing the size of the creature and the short distance they were from each other, the hunter knew that he would not have a chance to outrun it. He prayed for help, and about five minutes passed. Then the creature turned, walked away, and disappeared into the forest. The hunter, still frozen from fear and shock, was not able to move. He could still hear the sounds of breaking limbs and twigs from the gigantic footsteps of the creature as it walked away from him. After another twenty minutes had passed, when there was nothing but silence left, the hunter turned around and fled as fast as he could back to his truck. He has never stepped foot into that part of the woods again.

Although most cases of sightings of the Fouke Monster date from the early seventies forward, Fouke locals claim that the creature has haunted the area since the mid-sixties and that those sightings simply have not been reported to the media. Locals also report that the sightings date back as far as the mid-forties. Since the initial clusters of sightings during the seventies, there have been sporadic reports of the creature. In 1991, the creature was reportedly seen jumping from a bridge.

There were several reported sightings in 1997, and in 1998, the creature was supposedly spotted near a creek south of Fouke. More recent sightings from 2000 to 2010 were recounted in Lyle Blackburn's 2012 book, *The Beast of Boggy Creek: The True Story of the Fouke Monster.* The reason this creature hit so close to home for me was the fact that I grew up hearing stories about it. I was also raised on the cult film classic from 1972, *The Legend of Boggy Creek.* Much of the film was shot on location in Fouke, Texarkana, Arkansas, and in Shreveport, Louisiana. Many in the cast were local people or Texarkana college students. It was one of the very first docudramas about the topic.

After our conversations in the café, we asked how to find some of the hot spots of sighting locations. Carol was itching to go into the swampy woods. An adventurous soul, she was ready for some action. I personally wanted to receive a psychic perception about who and what this creature truly was. I knew that over the years it had been hunted—and even shot—so I did not want to investigate at that time with any intentions of invasion or disturbance. As we drove down a long and deserted-looking dirt road, I continually sent out signals of peace and communion. I wanted to send a telepathic message to the creature, "I come in peace." It was trite, but I did it anyway.

The time was an hour or so before evening. The sun was not yet setting. Driving deeper into the woods revealed a spooky environment that was somewhere between darkness and light. It was summertime, so it took longer for the evening to fully blanket the area. We parked the car by the edge of the woods and took a hiking trail deep into the swampy environment. It was humid, and the air was very thick. Not a soul was in sight, and the farther we went into the woods, the darker and quieter it became. I noticed that the crickets had begun to taper off their singing, and I had not heard any birds chirping for some time. My feeling was that things were about to get intense and very strange. My "Spider-sense" (from *Spider-Man*) was tingling. Something was watching us, and I felt it. I told Carol to stop walking, and we stood there in the woods, where the only sound was the creek water rolling in the distance. Not a living being was making any sound. Where was the wildlife? Even the summer breeze had abandoned us. We stood as still as statues.

The energy felt dense and extremely intense. Carol began to be frightened by the silence and the unknown sense of something watching us, but I knew that there was no danger. I closed my eyes and began to listen with my psychic sense. He's out there watching us. He's testing us. It's an energy he sends out to scare people away.

"He is not going to harm us."

Carol mumbled "uh huh" sarcastically under her breath.

I knew she had images of the two of us screaming and running for our lives through the dark woods, where tripping on a branch might be the end of us with the monster in pursuit.

"I promise," I whispered.

The energy of intensity began to taper off after the creature felt that we envisioned no harm. It was interesting because I knew he was nearby. I wondered why there were no significant skunk odors, a visual of the creature, or even some noise made by his footsteps as others had reported in their sightings. Bingo, the answer came to me as fast as I was asking the question, and suddenly a series of "downloads" began to run through my psychic files. First, the creature is an interdimensional being, and it has the ability to be invisible and psychically camouflage itself. As with other interdimensional beings, it can exist in a dimension beyond our own. These entities are able to manifest in physical and energetic forms and to travel between the supernatural realms via interdimensional doorways. This capability is one of the reasons why there has been no real evidence found of a Bigfoot corpse, so far.

Where was this information coming from, I wondered. I kept silent as the downloads kept coming into my mind. These particular creatures were living peacefully with nature long before humans evolved on the planet. They are unique beings and creatures, and they were once the guardians of the ecosystem in league with the Nature Realm. They love living on the earth and have chosen to remain hidden deep within underground hollows and caves. Even though they are interdimensional, they first lived on this planet and then made it their home. They are not extraterrestrial; they are children of Gaia. As the planet evolved, they were forced to literally choose hiding and invisibility. Over the years, they have popped in and out of dimensions, and that is when the sightings occur. They are still working with the Nature Realm to guard and protect the environment, but with the overpopulation of humans and their encroaching concrete-jungle lifestyle, these beings have and will remain just behind the veil. The Bigfoots are not generally enthralled by humans, but the Fouke monster seemed to be equally as curious about me as I was about him. I realized it was he who was sending me the information, and I wondered how long it had been since he had had a conversation with another living being? Suddenly the answer came again: all of these particular creatures are connected and communicate with each other. Telepathy was the normal communication system of the planet many eons ago. Humans have lost that ability, but the Bigfoot creatures still live and breathe the lifestyle of primordial times. I began to cry as I received a vision of what the earth looked like millions of years ago as opposed to what it looks like now.

The Bigfoot creatures are the most beautiful and peaceful beings I have ever had the honor to contact. The only time they seem aggressive is when humans draw near to their dwellings and families, when they have been known to react by screaming and throwing rocks. Some people have claimed attack, but I do not believe it. Those folks were most likely the attackers, or at least they appeared to threaten the creatures. As a child, I remembered having vivid dreams of these creatures living in actual villages underneath the earth. They were being invaded and I was a human who helped them to escape. I never really knew the origin of that dream. Maybe it was a remembrance of a time long ago, and my current reconnection with these beings was truly a reunion.

After some more deep breathing while I remained tranced out, Carol, who had been patiently waiting for a long time, said, "All right, let's get the hell out of here. It's getting dark."

I popped out of my dream state. *Thank you,* I said in my mind to the creature who was somewhere out there in the dense woods.

We walked back to the car; Carol kept looking back over her shoulder. She looked somewhat annoyed.

"What's wrong?" I asked.

"Oh, nothing—I'm just tired of your getting all the goods while I get nothing. I'm a visual person; I'd love to have seen the damned thing." Her head was down and her hands were in her pockets. If there had been a tin can around, she would have kicked it.

I chuckled and laughed. "I'm sorry." *What can you say in those situations?*

When we arrived at the car, Carol opened the driver's door and yelled into the oncoming darkness, "Thanks for nothing!"

She got into the car, and we closed the doors; rather, she slammed hers. Then, as both of us burst into laughter, she apologized for being childish, and we began to drive down the dirt road and back onto the highway. It was sunset, the perfect time between light and dark, and the sky revealed a deep blood-orange horizon. I began to share the information that Bigfoot had given me. Suddenly, just as we began to drive across a small bridge that crossed Boggy Creek, we saw it. Ahead of us on the other side of the bridge, the creature was standing on the side of the road. The hairy beast was huge! Carol slammed on the brakes, bringing the car to a halt in the middle of the bridge. We could not take our eyes away from it. The headlights exposed his dark red hair—bushy, matted, and filled with twigs and leaves. It felt as though his blood red eyes stared directly into our souls. Then, with a bolt and a sweeping step, he flashed across the road and seemed to disappear under the bridge where we were still sitting in the stopped car. We both looked at each other and simultaneously ran out of the car that was still running but parked in the middle of the bridge.

We ran over to the side of the bridge and looked down. Nothing was visible. We walked down to the creek, not realizing just yet the impact of what had happened and what might be waiting for us under the bridge. There was nothing. Bigfoot was gone. I don't think we took one breath throughout the entire ordeal. At this point, we realized it was probably wise to return to the car, ASAP. We got in, and Carol robotically began to drive down the road. Realization set in, and then Carol began to cry.

"Are you okay?" I asked.

"Yes, I just—. I'm—. Oh, hell, I don't know! It was amazing. He was amazing." Carol understood that the creature had heard her displeasure and had rewarded her with a visual. "It was so amazing," she repeated as she cried.

I smiled, mentally thanked the creature again, and once more offered a sigh of gratitude to the supernatural wonders of the universe as we headed down the road to Louisiana.

Mothman

A few years after the Bigfoot encounter, I was headlining on a speaking tour in Indianapolis, IN. I was staying with my friend Patsy, a born and bred Hoosier, until the end of my two-day workshop. Maryland was the next place where I was scheduled to speak. I really don't enjoy flying, so Patsy decided that she would drive me to Maryland. She had some vacation time and had always wanted to visit that part of the country. We settled in for a pleasant road trip and had a lot of fun on the way. A few days later, as we were making good time on our journey, we ended up in a little town called Eighty Four, PA. It was getting late and we were tired. We passed a place called the Avalon Motor Inn but decided to drive a little farther. Pennsylvania has a strange energy to it. It feels as though there are a dozen supernatural doorways all over the place. West Virginia is also extremely magnetic to supernatural occurrences, and that state was just a few hours away from where we were. If we had had more time, we would have stopped at the famous paranormal hot spot of Point Pleasant, West Virginia, home of the infamous Mothman.

Mothman is a legendary creature who was seen in the Point Pleasant area of West Virginia during the mid- to late sixties. There were countless eyewitness accounts and reports of the creature, and a Mothman book was introduced to the world in 1975—*The Mothman Prophecies* by John Keel. The book claimed that Mothman was related to various supernatural events in the Point Pleasant area and might have been the cause of the collapse of the Silver Bridge, which connected Point Pleasant, West Virginia and Gallipolis, Ohio, over the Ohio River. The 2002 film, *The Mothman Prophecies*, starring Richard Gere, was based on Keel's book. There are still Mothman encounters today. Paranormal authors and cryptozoologists believe that Mothman might be an alien, a supernatural being, or an unknown cryptid (loosely translated as a legendary creature not yet proven by science). Some folks claimed that the Point Pleasant residents experienced premonitions of the collapse of the Silver Bridge. Apparently, the residents also witnessed UFO sightings, threatening men in black, and other strange paranormal occurrences. Some even believe that the location was cursed by a Native American leader many years ago.

Several close encounters claim that the wings of Mothman were featherless. Even odder were the huge, red, glowing eyes on the face. Other eyewitnesses were unable to recall seeing a head at all; they claimed the eyes were actually in the shoulder area where a neck and head should have been. Other people who encountered this creature reported that it could fly without flapping its wings and could match the speed of a car racing at one hundred miles an hour. The creature never seemed to flap its wings when rising from the ground. It looked as if it were able to ascend in the air without any effort and without making any noise. I thought about how terrifying this spectacle must have been for people who actually experienced the presence of this relatively unknown supernatural species.

Until this point in time, I had done only minor research on this strange being, and I had not seen the movie. As we drove, I continued to ponder the Mothman and was lost in thought when I was interrupted by Patsy's announcement that we had arrived at our location. We pulled up to the hotel and settled in for the night. I *turned on the television, and lo and behold,* The Mothman Prophecies movie was playing. I had tuned in at the exact time where the Avalon Motor Inn, which we had just passed, was shown in the movie.

I looked at Patsy, who suddenly proclaimed loudly, "Oh, no! I'm not dealing with any Mothman craziness tonight. You just tell it to back off. Why does this stuff happen every time we get together?"

I laughed at the funny synchronicity of it all and went into the bathroom to brush my teeth. Patsy was correct; all my life I have experienced a pattern of bumping into the supernatural. The veil frequently seems to lift in my presence. I closed the bathroom door behind me and tried without success to find the light switch on the wall.

I was able to locate a pull string above the mirror, and suddenly there was light. The light bulb attached to the socket must have been 800 watts because it blinded me. I could hear that Patsy was still watching the Mothman movie in the background. There must have been a suspenseful moment in the film because I heard her say, "Good Lord!" She switched the channel to the news. Next, I heard an announcer advertising the Mothman festival that was coming up the next week in Point Pleasant.

Patsy shouted a few expletives and said, "We need to get out of here!"

The TV was turned off at that point, and I chuckled again. A Moth-man festival, I wondered. I had not even known that there was such a thing. All of this synchronicity was happening while I was quietly brushing my teeth, thinking nothing of the odd occurrences of the night concerning the Mothman.

As I was rinsing my mouth out, I suddenly experienced the particu-lar, strange Spider-sense that I develop when I'm being watched. The 800-watt light bulb began to flicker and I froze. I felt like there was static in the air, then all the air vanished, and I was in a soundless tunnel, ex-cept for the noise of static. I closed my eyes, and the static noise sounded very loud. I put my hand over my ears, and it became even worse. I began to try to breathe deeply, not knowing what the heck was going on. I immediately began to invoke the Archangel Michael for help. I knew this was a type of energetic interference, from something.

The next thing I knew, Patsy was banging on the bathroom door, screaming my name. "Darrin, are you okay? Are you okay?"

I looked around, and I was on the floor with a broken water glass beside me. The blazing 800-watt bulb was steadily burning and not flickering anymore. I gathered myself and realized the static noise was gone, too, thank God. I stood up, opened the door, and calmed Patsy down.

"What the hell happened? I heard a glass break and you falling."

"I don't know," I whispered.

"We are out of here," Patsy yelled.

She packed up our things and loaded the suitcases and me into the car before I knew it. We were on our way to Maryland, overnight. I did not completely come out of my fog until sunrise, and at that time, I realized I had a ringing in the ears. I had never had a ringing in my ears. I was able to get through my lecture in Maryland. When I returned home, I decided to get a medical check-up, even though I believed this occurrence had been something supernatural and not physical. My doctor was puzzled by my "fainting spell" and found no physical issues. He sent me home with a clean bill of health and a few remedies in hand. The remedies were herbal, of course; he knew my disdain for pharmaceutical medications. I had the ringing in the ears for at least a month before it grew quieter and quieter until it disappeared.

I have never been fearful when encountering anything paranormal or supernatural, but that incident caught me off guard and still puzzles me today. Bear in mind that I'm not at all afraid but just cautious when it comes to experiencing interdimensional entities. Was it the Mothman that ripped open the veil and stepped into the bathroom to assess me? Was I a light bulb for this moth creature? I believe that I did indeed attract Mothman to me. I was not attacked by this entity in any way; it was simply curious. I believe that Mothman is a curious interdimensional being that learns about us, tests our perceptual abilities, and uses them like a computer, at times. The being is energetic and it is also physical. It is the vibrational curiosity of intelligence that we are still questioning.

What is its origin? Is it an alien? No, I believe it's a creature of the multidimensional world; however, we may never really know. I feel that Mothman is not something to interfere with. It's a being that is comprised not of fear but not of love, either. It's impartial to our evolution as spiritual beings. I do believe that when I called the Archangel Michael for help, Mothman realized it was doing more harm than good to me and backed off—almost like saying, "Oops!" The creature is very scientific in its nature. Again, it did not back off from me as if to say, "Oh, sorry," but as a test of how much of its energy I could stand. That's my opinion about the Mothman, and perhaps someday I'll investigate it further. Currently, I'm satisfied with various theories about this creature. Even as I am writing this, I feel like Mothman is aware of my discussion of it.

UFOs and ETs

Personally, I have never been particularly interested in aliens, extraterrestrial beings (ETs), or unidentified flying objects (UFOs). I know that they are real and that they exist, but after eighteen years' experience with the New Age's obsession with ETs, I've become disenchanted. What I enjoy most about the whole subject is watching my gal pal, Dee Wallace, play the extraterrestrial's mother in the classic film from the eighties, *E.T. the Extra-Terrestrial*. Nevertheless, extraterrestrials are important, and as you know by now, I'll give you my thoughts and humble opinion about the subject.

My introduction into what I call the ET religion occurred in the mid-nineties. A friend of mine was intensely interested in ET contact and channelling. My red flags were up, so we agreed to disagree about this subject. She took me to a UFO conference in Eureka Springs, Arkansas. I entered the hotel conference hall and saw vendors selling alien T-shirts, alien contact spray (yes, a body spray to help make contact with aliens), and other ridiculous, cheap items. There were speakers lined up to talk about everything from alien abductions to alien babies and reptile people who were populating the earth. Honestly, I thought I was in Pee-wee Herman's playhouse. I exited early from one lecturer's talk; I guess that her discussion of having babies on a mother ship did not hold my interest! I walked out into the empty hotel lobby, grabbed a coffee, and enjoyed some peace and quiet away from the nutcases.

Sadly, my peace was disturbed by a crazy-looking hippy type of guy. He was holding something wrapped in a white sheet. He spotted me, and at that point I vocalized, quite loudly, "Oh, crap." He made a beeline for me.

"Hi," he said, with a crazy look in his eye.

"Hello," I said sternly, and with a bit of sarcasm.

"I have something you will want to see!"

I replied, "No, you don't."

The guy seemed to be extremely anxious. He unwrapped the sheet to reveal a peace of jagged-looking metal.

"These are pieces of a UFO, dude." He said, twitching.

"Dude, *really?*" I replied. My sarcasm can get the best of me.

He started laughing and walked away. Just then, as I was about to enjoy my newfound silence in the lobby, I spotted a tall, broad-shouldered man, dressed in a black suit with black sunglasses. *Really?* I thought. God, the lengths that some people will go to are incredible. The man dressed in black stood beside the pay phone—we had pay phones at that time. He was staring me down, and when I started feeling uncomfortable, I stood up to walk out the front door. He caught me before I could reach it.

"Excuse me," he said. His voice was deep and authoritative.

At this point, I was fed up with all of this UFO nonsense. I turned around and said, "*What?*"

He did not skip a beat as he grabbed my shoulder and asked, "Why are you here, Mr. Owens?"

"And who the hell are *you?*" I retorted, becoming exasperated as I shrugged his hand off of me.

"A simple question," he said.

"Get bent!" I said, and walked out.

I turned around as I walked away, and he was gone; the glass door was closed behind me. As I stepped outside and looked around, there was not a soul around. Then it dawned on me: *how did this guy know my name?* I went back to the hotel and waited for my friend. She arrived after the conference was over with an armful of bug-eyed ET dolls and books.

I dared not tell her of my encounter with the "man in black," because she would have gone nuts. It was around 5:00 in the afternoon, and it was time to head back to Little Rock, which was about a four-hour drive. We got into the car and for the next thirty minutes I heard about my friend's amazing time at the conference. She had the same crazy look in her eye. I wondered if all UFO groupies acquired that particular weird look. As we drove, I noticed a light up in the sky. The darker the sky became, the brighter that light became, and it seemed to follow the car. As I sped up, the light in the sky sped up, too. My friend noticed what I was doing and asked what was going on.

I said, "You are going to love this, but I think we are being followed." I pointed to the bright orb in the sky that was maintaining the exact speed we were driving.

"*Oh my God!*" she exclaimed.

We kept driving, and it followed us all the way to a rest stop.

We got out of the car, and it hovered. When I returned from the restroom, the darned thing was still there, in the same spot in the sky. We drove on, and it moved right along with us. My friend was quite excited; I thought she was going to explode.

"What do they want?" she kept repeating.

"I don't care!" I kept replying.

We made it back to Little Rock and I dropped her off. The orb was still high in the sky, waiting. I was hoping these beings were going to stay at my friend's house because she was just praying for abduction. No such luck—it followed me all the way to my house.

I stepped out of the car and shouted as I looked up, "I'll tell you what I told your man in black. Get bent!"

I walked into the house, watched some TV, and went to bed. I was woken up early in the morning by the sound of a helicopter. I walked outside into my yard and saw—you guessed it—a black helicopter circling my house. It circled three times and then flew away. I later learned from calling some reputable sources that these occurrences were attributes of UFO occurrences: men in black, black helicopters, and the unidentified light or object in the sky. It seemed that, like it or not, the UFO phenomenon was encroaching on my peaceful, psychic life. I much prefer interaction with ghosts, demons, and other supernatural disturbances, and this area of aliens did not hold my interest. Nevertheless, for some reason it had an interest in me.

Years later, other interesting extraterrestrial occurrences took place. In 2004, I finished working as a contract agent for the actress Shirley MacLaine. The opportunity of working with Ms. MacLaine enabled me to have deep discussions with UFO experts and investigators in the field. I found the world of ETs and UFOs to be interesting but still not especially stimulating. There seemed to be a huge cloud consisting of conspiracy theories and outrageous new age teachings of ascension and channellings that was too fluffy for my taste. Again, I could not see how any of these ideas actually helped people to live in the here and now and on this planet. We had enough spiritual mysteries occurring right here on earth. Why catapult ourselves into outer space with aliens that may or may not be in sync with our spiritual evolution, or even with our own planet earth? Many alien worshippers I'd met had a strange look in their eyes, similar to the look of those who had attended the UFO conference I had experienced. There were a few fans who seemed very levelheaded.

As time passed, I worked with other UFO leaders such as Dolores Cannon. She is a renowned past life expert who works with extraterrestrials in her healing hypnosis workshops. Again, I was a bit surprised to hear some fairly spaced-out information coming through some of these teachings that seemed to fluff the ego more than the spirit. This is just my humble opinion. At one of Dolores's events, I met Giorgio Tsoukalos of the History Channel's *Ancient Aliens* series. We were both headlining at this particular speaking event, and I found him to be the most grounded so far on the subject of ETs. Giorgio's ideas about the possibility that ancient astronauts influenced our planet's history and archaeological discoveries seemed very plausible. Even though the information and discussions were fascinating, I never jumped on that mother ship.

I saw more damage than good when it came to overzealous people jumping into the subject of ETs and their contact with them. These space men seem to have become another form of a messiah to some, and more and more people appear to lose their roots here on earth as they reach to the stars for their answers.

Again, these are just my thoughts and experiences. I agree that some of these star beings might be trying to help us, but I have found that our own internal guidance and spiritual guardians here on earth are all we need. As far as my experiences with the man in black and the "follow-the-leader" game with the UFO that night, I have no real answers. I have come close to some answers by understanding another interdimensional being that might be behind this topic.

Shadow People and the Djinn Phenomena

My friend and colleague Rosemary Ellen Guiley has spearheaded the research and investigation into other interdimensional phenomena of the supernatural, known as the Shadow People and the djinn. I first met Rosemary at an event where she was speaking in Ohio. We had talked on the phone and shared emails previously, and I was excited to connect with her in person. Rosemary Ellen Guiley is one of the leading experts on the paranormal with more than fifty published books. I had been reading her works for years. Some of the subjects that Rosemary was speaking on at this event concerned interdimensional portals, Shadow People, and spiritual creatures I had not been very familiar with, the djinn. My assistant Carol and I sat near the back of the conference room, and as Rosemary began to speak about the phenomena of the Shadow People, once again I began to feel my Spider-sense wake up.

Something was in the room, and it was apparently investigating the workshop.

I looked toward the back of the conference hall, and even though my physical eyes saw nothing, I knew there was something, or a group of something, watching the lecture. It was almost the same feeling as my encounter with "something" in Mothman country. Thank goodness there was no static noise, nor did I experience a blackout as I had in the hotel bathroom with Mothman. After the event and at dinner, I asked Rosemary about the visitation. She had also noticed the arrival of "them" at the lecture. I was glad to have this sense confirmed.

I learned that because of the research Rosemary has done and the revelations she has brought to the surface about these beings, they seem to check in on her—watching, assessing, and giving off the vibe that they don't like the veil being lifted away from their identities. So, who or what are these beings and what's their intention? Before I go any further, I want to recommend Rosemary's books that detail this subject: *Rosemary Ellen Guiley's Guide to the Dark Side of the Paranormal* and *The Djinn Connection: The Hidden Links between Djinn, Shadow People, ETs, Nephilim, Archons, Reptilians and other Entities*. Both books are published by Visionary Living, Inc. and can be found on Rosemary's Web site at www.VisionaryLiving.com.

Shadow People

I have had encounters with Shadow People since I was a young lad. When I was around seven and eight years old, I vividly remember waking up in the middle of the night and seeing two human-shaped forms that were dark figures standing in my bedroom. The air seemed to have left the room, and it was hard to breathe. I was able to jump up and run like heck with my eyes closed right through them, down the hallway and into my mother's bedroom, screaming about the men in my room! Of course, nothing was there when the light was turned on. The presence of these dark figures in my bedroom happened on and off until I was about fifteen and began to follow a more spiritual quest in my life. For some reason it stopped at that time. I also had clients and others tell me about their own encounters with Shadow People, and all were terrifying.

After dinner was over, Rosemary and I said our goodbyes with a mutual interest in more collaboration of the supernatural kind for the future.

When I returned to my apartment in Little Rock, the dog sitter had good reports on my little dog Tobey. She left and the pup and I got ready for bed. I was dog-tired, no pun intended, and fell asleep quickly. Before I knew it, I was woken up by the deep growl of my little dog.

Tobey was on the bed and was staring straight ahead. I looked up, and there were two very tall, humanoid shadow figures. The air felt thick, and I recalled that these were the same entities of my childhood memories that had invaded my peace when I was younger. I was not at all fearful, nor was I in a panic. I was not feeling the sense of being frozen, either, as some others had reported in their interactions with these shadow specters. I pulled my talisman out from under my shirt—it is one that I wear all the time—the shield of Solomon.

The moment I revealed my talisman, the figures seemed to be agitated. They began to look blurry. (Their first manifestation was pitch-black, with sharp outlines of silhouetted human figures.)

I boldly stated out loud, "You are not allowed here."

I began to pray the Lord's Prayer and called the Archangel Michael. They shuddered some more and then blinked out. I literally blinked my eyes and they were gone. I intuitively knew that these were the same beings that had visited Rosemary's lecture. It was around 3:15 in the morning, which was no surprise. Between 3 and 4 a.m. are extremely powerful times for supernatural activity. The veil is thinnest at that time. I decided to get up and make some coffee. I called Rosemary the next day, and she confirmed that my conclusion was correct and that they were checking in with me. Anytime these beings are discussed, especially among those who are working hard to notify the public of their existence, we will be placed on a watch list.

The next morning like clockwork at 3:15 a.m., Tobey growled, and there they stood. Again, I showed my talisman and said some prayers, and it was not long before they retreated. Other people who have had these encounters have reported a sense of tremendous fear, dread, and physical paralysis from these entities. Fear seems to be their method of manipulation and their power. In Rosemary's book, *Rosemary Ellen Guiley's Guide to the Dark Side of the Paranormal*, she describes in detail the characteristics of the Shadow People. Her research and thousands of reports from firsthand accounts have provided a little larger peek behind the veil into the world of the Shadow People.

> *There are different types of Shadow People. The core, dominant experience is the nighttime bedroom visitor: a tall silhouette of a man, often dressed in a coat or cape, and a brimmed hat. The figure is blacker than black and*

3-D, obstructing light and blocking the view of objects. There are no facial features or eyes (sometimes red eyes are reported), but the experiencer knows he is being observed with great intensity. The figures do not communicate, but often radiate a malevolent, trickster, or evil intent. Some people feel threatened by the Shadow Person. It sits on the bed, or presses on them, making them feel as though they will suffocate or choke. The experience ends before actual physical harm occurs, but the lingering terror takes a severe psychological toll. Some Shadow People are less formed and are more like pillars or vertical blobs of black. Other kinds of Shadow People start as shadows on the wall. It takes a moment for a person to realize that the shadow is unnatural and should not be there—and then the shadow starts to move. It materializes from the wall into physical space.

Shadow People also have been reported in wooded areas. In America, accounts of them go back to old Indian lore. They always seem to be watching . . . for something. Another category of Shadow People are dark figures seen in some haunted places. Waverly Hills Sanatorium in Louisville, Kentucky and Eastern State Penitentiary in Philadelphia are famous for them. These figures are believed to be dark ghosts or thought-forms that are part of the haunting phenomena present on site. (Rosemary Ellen Guiley's Guide to the Darkside of the Paranormal, *56-57*)

So, what are these beings? First, from my experience and interpretation of my own encounters, I do not believe that they are ghosts, demons, or thought forms. They have intelligence. I don't believe they are ETs, either. I know that they are interdimensional beings. Even though I had my Solomon's shield talisman and invoked the Lord's Prayer, the Shadow People did not retreat or react as most demonic energies do. In addition, they appeared again. I believe they knew that I did not and do not fear them, so they left me alone—at least for the time being!

Don't get me wrong, I'm still in my spiritual power and know that they cannot harm me without a major psychic fight that would put Harry Potter to shame, but they are definitely interested in tracking those that research and investigate them. Another point Rosemary makes in her book is that: *"Shadow People may be unknown beings from other dimensions that layer ours, an explanation posed for mysterious creatures such as Mothman and Bigfoot. They do seem to slide at will between our world and theirs.* (Rosemary Ellen Guiley's Guide to the Darkside of the Paranormal, 61)

The Djinn

Rosemary Guiley has delved into some fascinating research on the connection between Shadow People and the djinn. Also, there seems to be a hint that these particular supernatural curiosities may be linked to what lies behind the ET and UFO mysteries. The djinn are not very well known here in the West but are quickly becoming a hot new research topic for paranormal investigators. As we understand more about what's living behind the veil, we are learning about what is truly stepping through it and affecting our world. How does that saying go—"curiosity killed the cat"? I don't believe that our curiosity will kill us, but I do know that what we are discovering will eradicate many long-believed theories about the supernatural.

Let me return to writing about the djinn. In the folklore of the Arabian Nights, the djinn were considered to be genies. And I'm not talking about the bouncy genie represented by Barbara Eden (from *I Dream of Jeannie*). These significant, supernatural entities were born of smoke and fire.

The djinn exist within interdimensional realms and are fierce. We can also find the history of them in the tales of the powerful magician and spiritual master, King Solomon. God granted Solomon charge over spirits and animals, and he had the djinn bound and enslaved. They were frisky creatures, so it was for the safety of everyone that Solomon used his God-given power to keep these beings at bay. This information is not a story from the Holy Bible. This legend is found in more occult writings such as the Testament of Solomon, an Old Testament work credited to King Solomon of Jerusalem. It describes how Solomon, using a magical ring entrusted to him by the Archangel Michael, was authorized to build his temple by commanding demons. This ancient text dates somewhere between the first and fifth centuries AD, and the author or authors of the text are unknown. If you want the good stuff, always research the spiritual mysteries in these sacred writings that are rather hidden and definitely not on the current best seller list. So, the story goes that the "demons" Solomon had control over were actually the djinn. This account explains why the Shadow People seemed to blur and become agitated when I pulled out my Solomon's shield. Perhaps the talisman elicited bad memories from their past?

There seems to be a link between the djinn phenomena and the Shadow People. As the story goes, within the religious texts of Islamic belief systems, the djinn were created by God from smoke and fire, angels were created from spiritual light, and humans were created from clay and earth. The folk legends state that the djinn and the angels were created before man and that when God created man, he commanded the angels and the djinn to bow down to his new creations. The angels did as they were told with great compassion. The djinn, for the most part, did not like this new heavenly direction whatsoever and rebelled. I love the way this story reflects the Christian story of the fall of Satan from the realm of the heavens. Worldwide, all legends have similar foundations of truth.

As we look back to Solomon, he had the power to bind the djinn and command them to do his bidding, keeping them out of the human realm. Of course, I have read these stories with my own interpretation and believe that when Solomon died, the djinn were liberated and went on the warpath.

As you read this information, you may think it's too far-fetched and not really applicable to the paranormal activity happening today, but I beg to differ. Especially with the onset of countless people who are having encounters with the Shadow People, the link between those encounters and the legends of the djinn seems to be evident in black and white. Could there be a link between the djinn and the Shadow People? The ancient hidden ones who live behind the veil seem to have great interest in our world, and as the lore says, they lost it to us. Was it a djinn that I encountered near Point Pleasant, West Virginia that night in the hotel bathroom? And what about the ET connection between the djinn and the Shadow People? Some believe that these extraterrestrial entities are casting everyone's eyes to the sky to distract what's really going on behind the veil here on earth. Some also say that the ETs connect with the interdimensional beings here on earth for research purposes. Okay, okay! You, dear reader, might be thinking: *Darrin has lost it. He has gone out on a limb, fallen off, and hit every branch on the way down.* Yes, I admit that perhaps this topic stimulates me to be as passionate as the UFO folks I was making fun of earlier. But we must not keep our minds closed to the wonders and mysteries behind the veil. The research has really just begun on this aspect of the supernatural and the multidimensional beings that inhabit it. Even though we may not know exactly who or what these entities are or what they want, we are confident that we are spiritual beings created by God. We have learned that without fear, we can remain strong and secure when we encounter *anything*. I'm leaving you with a question mark here for this chapter. The reason is that this chapter is not meant to answer the question of *who* or *what* are any of these beings I have mentioned.

I want you to keep questioning and searching for your own truth in this area. I myself am still investigating and researching these elusive intelligences and am kicking up my heels regarding the results. I have added a list of books at the end of this book for you to read and discover more about what I have discussed. As they say, "Seek and you will find."

The Paranormal Realm

The Paranormal Realm is the most popular of all realms these days, it seems. The saturation of paranormal reality shows on television, complete with their scripted nonsense and lack of reverence, provides the general public with a very sad view on an amazing and beautiful realm of the supernatural. I have absolutely no respect for these reality shows or the television addicts who watch them. Commercializing and monopolizing on the dead is an abomination in my eyes.

A year ago, I spoke at a paranormal convention. The host is a wonderful friend and has the same respect for those that have passed on as I do. The Friday night before the actual event, there was a "meet and greet" with all the speakers. My husband, my assistant, and I showed up at the MacArthur Museum of Arkansas Military History in Little Rock, Arkansas. This paranormal expo was a charity event for the museum, so I was ready and willing to be a speaker and participate. Arkansas history is a passion for me. It was around 8:30 at night, and the darkness had already crept in around the large stone building—a perfect setting for an episode of *American Horror Story*. As we walked up the steps to the front gallery, I looked up to the tower of the building and noticed on the second floor an old man staring back at me. It was obviously a ghost; but more than that, it was a ghost with an attitude!

He gave me his haunting stare and shook his head as if to say, *don't even think about coming up here.*

"No problem," I replied aloud. My husband and my assistant are used to my talking to the thin air. "We are not to go into the tower," I said.

"Okay," the gang agreed. They know to listen when I get my prophetic visions.

All the speakers gathered in the main hall of the building. It was like a carnival show. A few folks from the SyFy TV channel were there with all their reality show memorabilia, along with other local Arkansas paranormal groups. We were all introduced and then there was to be a group investigation. I chose not to participate in the investigation but did warn the others of the old man upstairs who did not want company.

One gal who claimed to have invented an anti-ghoul spray that banished ghosts (according to the business card that she shoved at me) announced that the old man specter had been the head of the building some time ago, and they should get a really good EVP and orb photo from this exploration.

"Did you hear what I just said?" Most of the folks just ignored my warning.

The host knew better and kept herself out of it. The "ghoul go-away" gal snickered and bounced away.

I, with my big mouth, voiced quite loudly, "By the way, ghouls are not ghosts." Sometimes I can't help myself.

My party and I left for the night. The next morning, there was quite a buzz from the activity that had transpired the night before.

The host of the event rushed up to me and said, "Darrin, you were right! Last night, the group went upstairs to the second floor of the tower. Two women fell violently ill, and another member of the group saw a black orb hovering over the two that became sick."

"Well, duh," I replied. When it comes to the supernatural, you will get bitten if you don't have the sense that God gave a church mouse!

Respect and compassion for the dead is the first and foremost rule to remember when you are dealing with this realm. Even nasty spirits lived human lives. They deserve a chance for salvation and liberation into the light.

The Paranormal Realm exists between the Nature Realm and the Spiritual Realm. It is the realm that every soul passes through on the way to the Spiritual Realm. The tunnel of light that is seen during out-of-body experiences and at the time of physical death is the thoroughfare that a soul can choose to enter into another dimension. There are various tunnels and doorways to all realities of the supernatural. When souls choose not to take the tunnel to the Spiritual Realm, they become earthbound. They become lost in the darkness and psychic mist of the

Paranormal Realm. Think of yourself going to the train or bus station. Sadly, you missed your transportation, so you are stuck in the busy terminal. The Paranormal Realm is just like that.

A few years ago, I decided to take a train trip to Oregon. My soon-to-be husband was there, and I thought it would be a great idea to jump aboard from Arkansas to take a four-day trip to reconnect with him. I had a good seven-hour layover at Union Station in Los Angeles, CA. It was packed with people. Most people looked like zombies who were locked in their own minds and their own realities. Some folks were in happy moods; some were not. Almost everyone looked stuck and with no realization that anyone else was around him or her. It reminded me very much of what the Paranormal Realm must be like when a soul is cemented in it.

Hauntings occur when a lost soul or ghost chooses not to leave a certain area or location. Sometimes they don't even know that they are dead. They loom around as if they are in a perpetual dream state. Sometimes the living and the dead are able to interact with each other, and that's when a paranormal disturbance occurs. I was called into a case some years ago about a disturbance at a tiny farmhouse in the delta region of Arkansas. When I arrived, I could feel a definite presence in the back bedroom. It was the children's room. When I tapped in, I could feel the presence of a young African American woman. She was very protective of the children, and for the past several months since they had moved in, she had rattled the place to its foundation. Lights had been switched on and off, doors slammed shut, and toys thrown across the room. The parents had been the main target.

Like clockwork, just as the father and mother were about to doze off to sleep, something would shatter or fall in the house. Something wanted to turn their silent night into a loud and chaotic one. One day when one of the children was acting up, the mother punished the child and took away her teddy bear. After the child calmed down, she would be allowed to have it back. The mother placed the bear on the top of the refrigerator. Then she walked back into the living room to pick up some dirty dishes. She returned to the kitchen not even five minutes later and noticed that the bear was gone.

The mother looked everywhere for it and realized that maybe her child had it. But how? She was only three years old, and there was no way she could reach the very top of the refrigerator. The mother walked back to the child's bedroom to ask her if she might know where the bear went. As the mother entered the room, she noticed that her daughter was fast asleep on her bed with her arms wrapped around the bear. Incidents like that began to be a daily occurrence.

When I walked into the bedroom, I immediately made contact with the spirit. Of course, I could tell that this lady was no fan of men.

"What do you *want*? I'm here to help," I communicated.

"You be gone, leave us be."

I knew that she was talking about the children she had attached herself to and herself. As some of you might know, I get right to the point.

"Lady, do you realize you're dead? You are no longer part of the world." Suddenly I began to have a hell of a headache, and I was no longer in the bedroom. I felt like I was in a dream state.

I was outside of the little farm house now, and I could tell that it was many years earlier—perhaps the early fifties. I saw the African American woman walking up the path.

I was living in some kind of alternate dream state. It was like watching a movie. She was singing sweetly and entered the tiny house. As the vision continued, I saw that she was actually a housemaid to the family who lived in the house during that time. The house was happy, full of love, and she loved those kids. Her name was Adina. Suddenly the picture changed, and it was later in the day. Adina had left the house for the day. It was already dark. She continued up the country road. From a distance, I could see a farmhand's small shack in the field. I knew that was where she lived with her family. Then a truck raced up the road and skidded to a stop right in front of Adina's path. Three men jumped out and began to chase her into the fields. All three were Caucasian. I saw her fall, I saw them beating her in the head with steel pipes, and then it was over. I was suddenly back in the room, in the present.

The team I was with stood around me and tried to hold me up. I was still in contact with Adina's soul, and as I was watching, her spirit was watching, too. After they killed her, she walked back to the tiny farmhouse in her spiritual form and had never left. It was where she felt most comfortable. It was safe and happy for her. She had been haunting this location since the early fifties. When souls experience a traumatic death, it can be so violent that they literally pop out of their body before they know what's actually happening. Poor Adina was killed because of pure racial hatred, nothing more.

As a healer, this kind of occurrence will happen frequently. The fact is, when I help a family or an individual with a haunting, the healing often goes both ways. Adina began to open her sleepy eyes and realize that she was in another dimension.

Time in the Paranormal Realm means nothing. As we know, time is a man-made device. Once you cross the waters into the Paranormal Realm or any of the supernatural realms, all physical laws are null and void. To Adina, it seemed like just another day at the little farmhouse. As I communicated more with her and calmed her down, she conveyed that it was odd that the other family had moved away so quickly. She did not like this present family. The parents ignored her, but the children often played with her. As we conversed, she also revealed to me that the husband was a drunkard—in her words—and screamed at the mother and the kids. When the father started in on his drunken rants, Adina would shove things off the counter and turn lights on and off. At bedtime, what looked like a chaotic intention to keep the parents awake was in fact a request for them to stop arguing so the children could sleep. After another thirty minutes of ghost therapy, I was able to help Adina over into the Spiritual Realm. I promised I would talk to the parents and also ensure that the children would be unharmed. Adina learned that after she crossed over, she could choose to come back as a protector spirit for the kids for as long as they needed her help. This possibility was wonderful news to me, as well. When I work with lost souls who need to cross over, I work with a group of spiritual intelligence that I lovingly call the "Band of Mercy."

The Band of Mercy helps me in my spiritual deliverance work. They are ancestors of spiritual guides and loving souls that have chosen to work between the Paranormal Realm and the Spiritual Realm in helping lost souls to awaken and go home. They communicated to me that Adina could be charged as the children's protecting guide, and this news warmed my heart.

After Adina crossed over, I walked into the living room where the parents were waiting as if to hear some bad news from a doctor.

Again, getting right to the point, I said, "So, Father, let's talk about this drinking problem."

His face went white, and the wife gasped.

"I also hear that you participate in drunken shouting matches with everyone in the house."

He opened his mouth and his head fell into his hands. The next two hours brought family therapy, communication, and healing. Things have changed in this house even to this day, and knowing that Adina would be watching was also a great catalyst to maintain balanced conditions. Healing goes both ways in a situation like this one. Lost souls are only lost because they have forgotten the spiritual heritage that is waiting for them. Just as we in the physical world can get lost on our path, the same is true for those out of body. This story is an example of why I desperately want to wake people up to that fact that those in the Paranormal Realms are not playthings to shake a flashlight at or poke at with a talking board during a slumber party. The biggest disrespect arises from the commercialization of the dead by television mediums and ghost hunters making millions of dollars for sensational purposes. Despicable!

Honoring the Ancestors:
Respect for and Blessing the Dead

The power and presence of the dead is very sacred. Most of us regard speaking to the dead as entertainment, nowadays. I have always advocated against mediumship as a parlor game or celebrity psychics with certificates for their psychic powers. There is a vast difference in talking to the dead in a complete process and then working with them in an ancestral manner. Native American, African, New Orleans Voodoo, and southern Hoodoo traditions all carry strong connections to the dead as a spiritually protective relationship. There is a misperception about some of these traditions regarding the belief that they "worship the dead." This idea is a great falsehood. There is a communion and work to be done with these souls, but the power behind their blessing is that of God.

Many other religious paths have various ways of honoring and working with the ancestors such as working with the saints and masters. Catholics petition saints to aid them in their spiritual healing and everyday events and circumstances. Saints are very much a part of the honoring process. They, too, were once living and breathing on this earth and are now charged with the sacred task of helping humans on this side of the veil. Our elders and family members who have passed on can also be empowered by the spirit of God to aid us. Even ancestors that may not be a part of our own biological tribe can enter into our lives on God's command to direct us. Many people create altars to honor their dead—to pray for them or to petition their help. In the new age community, the process is similar to asking a spirit guide for help. Later in the book, I'll write about altar work and the importance of having one in your home.

Ever since I was young, I can remember one ancestral being that has always been around me. It was not until just recently from research for this book and from my own personal spiritual education that I happened upon this ancestor as an actual guide and protector. Her name was La Madama. Folk legend has it that La Madama is the spirit of an old slave woman who had been a conjure woman and spiritual healer. Old-fashioned "Aunt Jemima" pancake mix advertising art or "Mammy" style cookie jar figures are images often used to represent La Madama. When I found out about La Madama from my research, I was astonished, as I have had these figurines in every place I have lived. I have always felt protected and safe—funny to say, but true—when these little icons were around.

La Madama is often depicted with a broom—a tool symbolic of cleansing away negativity. She is also believed to be a guiding force for psychic readers and practioners. She is a "tell it like it is" guide, which is perfect for me. These ancestral energies are souls that have crossed into the depths of the Paranormal Realm and have been initiated into the Spiritual and Divine Realms as guides and guardians. They can return to our world for our guidance and support. They are always looking out for our spiritual well-being and are ready to be of assistance. For further reading, there are more comprehensive works on this subject in the recommended reading list at the back of this book.

Mediumship, Spirit Contact, and the Paranormal

We are all intrigued by life after death. For centuries, our fascination with the spirit world (or the Paranormal Realm) has filtered into our culture through books, movies, television, and religious beliefs. Spiritualism in the eighteen hundreds marked a great jump in popularity though mediumship. In those days, just like today, it was rare to find an authentic medium. Most of the time, the fakes used plenty of smoke and mirrors. Currently, mediums seem to have big hair, a New Jersey accent, and long nails. Mediumship has become a circus act. A unique ability has changed from a gift to a marketable commodity. These days, the real deals—the genuine mediums—have to suffer the reality show façade that has been created by others.

The power of mediumship is that of a spiritual gift. A medium is someone who can "communicate with the dead" as well as swim within the realms of the paranormal and the spiritual. Mediumship is a part of our spiritual nature. I'm not talking about how to take a class on "Mediumship 101." I'm talking about authentic communion with the paranormal using respect, honor, and dignity. I have been very staunch in my teachings on mediumship. Most of the time, I do not believe that people are spiritually mature enough to accept and understand what is real about it. They look at mediumship as a special power to acquire, become certified in, and then employ by hanging out a shingle. Where is the spiritual foundation here? Where is the true meaning of it all? I have noticed that most folks who call themselves mediums can't even begin to navigate the different realms. There is a lack of respect and definitely a lack of discernment.

One day, a call came into my office from a group of college kids who were at a cemetery. The guy on the mobile phone was hysterical. It was actually around 10:30 at night, and I was still awake when the office phone rang. I usually don't answer calls after five p.m., but something told me to pick this one up. The poor college kid was crying. When I had calmed him down, he finally communicated that he and three of his friends were using a Ouija board in the old town cemetery. One of his friends during the "do-it-yourself" séance became ill and passed out. The other guy experienced a sudden sense of hysteria. It was at that moment when the third kid searched the Internet via his mobile phone and found me. Luckily, they had all left the cemetery and were departing in the car as they called me. They were afraid that whatever "hit" them would follow. I said my deliverance prayer, and they began to calm down. I allowed them to come to my office for further help.

As all three guys sat on my couch, cold and a bit calmer, I interrogated them. I found out that they had taken a class taught by a well-known, self-proclaimed medium. They were told that for practice, they could go to the cemetery with a talking board to sharpen their spiritual communication skills. *Really?*

In addition, they decided to have a few beers before setting up the spirit chat. To begin with, I have never approved of using any kind of spirit board or spirit communication device unless there is a skilled, authentic teacher present for guidance. Most of the time, I advise people to be cautious and not to bother with those things. I know only a few folks in my profession who could actually teach authentic spirit board techniques. They are shamans and hoodoo practitioners, so there is much more to it than asking simple yes or no questions.

So these three kids, not really knowing what they were doing, took a spirit talk board to an old cemetery. There they drank up a few spirits, so to speak, and had the nerve to demand communication with the dead. Of course, they experienced unexpected effects!

Their disrespect and lack of discernment sent something on the warpath, which "kicked their astral." As I sat and listened to their story, seething, I heard a voice.

It said, "They are not welcome."

Okay, I thought. "Who's this?" I said aloud.

The boys stopped talking and watched me like deer frozen by a car's headlights.

"Who is this?" I asked once again.

"The Guardian of the Graves."

"Holy hell," I said.

I learned that there is a guardian at every gravesite—a protector. It has the job of tending to the dead who are still at their graves. This information was truly news to me, but the Guardian of the Graves came and went so quickly that I did not have a chance to interview it. I have often thought of going back to the old town cemetery with appropriate respect to see if the guardian would tell me more about its job. And I will. Nevertheless, the boys entered a space of hallowed ground with no respect, and they paid the price. Intuition told me that graveyards are sacred because they are vortexes or tunnels to the Paranormal and Spiritual Realms. The Guardian of the Graves is the gatekeeper. The first thought that comes to mind is that of a security guard. They open and shut the door. Being different from the Band of Mercy, the guardian keeps the peace. This story shows why it's so important to have respect for the dead. When you have respect, compassion, and a sense of sacredness, you will attract those types of spirits. But if you have the opposite attitudes, you will draw that same kind of vibration from the Paranormal Realm.

Many of us seem to wonder about the power of talking to the dead. It's a supernatural feat that seems to be given to a select few, but in reality it's an aptitude that we are born with and are able to do. The reason we are so drawn to life beyond this one is the fact that we know what's there. It's not a mystery. I think the wonder is misplaced, and there should be a sense of knowing. We fear death because we are attached to the physical realm. I have softened my approach to the subject of mediumship since my last book, *Becoming Masters of Light*. Working in the new age and self-help genre for eighteen years damaged my perception when it came to mediumship. The hype, the reality shows, and the sense of self-absorbed power in people's eyes when they left "mediumship" class bothered me. Most of the possession cases that I had dealt with for a long time were due to acts of stupidity similar to the behavior of the kids in the cemetery. I now realize as I study for my own personal, spiritual education that an understanding of our ancestors and a sincere respect for the dead changes the entire picture. Meeting the "grave guardian" and learning of my own ancestral guides gave me a completely new perspective on meduimship and contact with the dead. God himself has obviously set up parameters for the care of all souls that are lost or travelling to another destiny. If we show that same respect and compassion, we will be able to understand and communicate with the dead, led by God to a higher wisdom. We will not regard mediumship as a special psychic power but as a spiritual lifestyle.

When it comes to the Paranormal Realm, as Forrest Gump would say, it's like a box of chocolates, and you never know what you're going to get. The Paranormal Realm is a soup bowl of different beings, all with different backgrounds and intentions. With a heart aligned with the Divine, you will be able to work and commune with those of the same vibration. Show disrespect, and you may find the Guardian of the Graves on your heels!

The Spiritual Realm

We are surrounded not only by beings of the Paranormal Realm but also by those of the Spiritual Realm. The Spiritual Realm enables souls that have died to cross over to their next life, destiny, and direction. The tunnel-of-light concept provides access—a doorway—to a higher plane of existence beyond the Paranormal Realm. Within the Spiritual Realm are our ancestral guides, family, and friends who have passed on, and other spiritual directors, also. Think of the Spiritual Realm as the administrative offices you pass through before you encounter the bigwigs of the supernatural area, the head offices of the Divine Realm. This realm is where we go to learn more about who we are as children of the most high. Learning centers, healing centers, and sanctuaries are also part of the Spiritual Realm.

During my readings with different individuals over the years, I have gleaned much of this information. It has emerged by understanding connections to their deceased loved ones who conveyed the information to me. In addition, good old-fashioned insight sculpted many of the details of the Spiritual Realm for me. The beings that successfully cross over into the Spiritual Realm are known as spirits. If souls are lost, stuck, or simply refuse to go into this realm, they are lost souls or ghosts who haunt the Paranormal Realm. Discernment is so very important when it comes to perceiving the supernatural in order to know with what and to whom you are communicating. There will be an invocation for discernment in a later chapter of this book.

The Spiritual Realm, although busy, is a very peaceful and relaxed place. Remember, there is no time, so there is no such thing as rushing. We come home to this place as spirits to learn more about our past lives, efforts toward healing, and spiritual destinies. If souls had a difficult

time with forgiveness in the last life, here they will have the opportunities to expand their knowledge on the subject. If two lovers were parted
by death, it is here that they can eventually reunite and combine forces
again. I have been asked over and over what we look like "over there."
Well, when souls have passed the river of life into the Spiritual Realm,
they look like themselves in their last life—except healthy and radiant.
Do we all look thirty years old? One self-made psychic created that big
idea some years ago. Please note that if spirits want to connect with you
beyond the veil for any reason, they will accommodate themselves to
your memory of them. If your eighty–year-old grandfather passed away
and chooses to look like he did in his thirties in the Spiritual Realm, he
can do that. But when he visits you from the other side, he looks like
he's eighty. Why? Because, that's how you knew him. If he showed up
looking like a thirty–year-old man, you might not know who he was.

There are teachers and guides in the Spiritual Realm who hold charge
over our learning process and teach us to use our full spiritual potential.
When we are living as a physical body and in a physical landscape,
working with our spiritual power is a bit more challenging, but there
are no limits or controls in the Spiritual Realm. When we die, we don't
just leave our physical body and float to heaven with angel wings and a
miniature harp, as depicted years ago by Warner Bros. Cartoons, Inc. We
will experience a deepening. Death is merely a deepening of a spiritual
process that is individualized for each soul.

During this spiritual process, there are various places souls can dwell
to advance their education. If souls have had a traumatic death or a
very problematic and challenging life, they may want to spend time in
the sanctuaries or healing centers of the Spiritual Realm.

On the subject of a difficult life, I'm often asked about souls and
the act of suicide. When people choose to kill themselves, ninety–nine
percent of the time they have become lost or stuck in their own depression. Souls that have left their physical bodies by their own hands are
very hard to "wake up" from their own misery. They usually wander
and worry and haunt the Paranormal Realm without any notice of the
doorways to the Spiritual Realm. Over time, these lost souls can become
vengeful spirits if not rescued. I have been able to rescue three soul
suicides in my entire career, and the others I have been in contact with
simply would not wake up. Please don't worry for these souls; they

have their own spiritual support checking in from time to time to nudge them toward a higher direction. In my spiritual belief system, all souls will return at some point to God, the source from which they came.

Another question I receive is: do we still reincarnate? My personal insight is that *no*, most of us in this present time will not incarnate back to this earth. Some souls with very heavy emotional baggage will reincarnate, but most will not. I feel it's because most of us will be spiritual guides for those new souls who are currently populating the earth. There is a fluffy new age belief that these new souls are higher beings of some sort, or evolved souls. Some may be. Nevertheless, I think that technology will override itself with help from many of the new souls that are too technologically advanced for their own good. They will need all the help they can get returning to the old ways—the ways of the earth and the root of spiritual power. Nothing beats the basics. That's just my two cents' worth, or my opinion on the subject. There are many so-called indigo children and rainbow children who attend my events, and parents often ask about the potential of their children who might be special. Let me kick that pedestal out from under anyone, right now. I don't buy into the separatist belief of special crystal, rainbow, or indigo children.

I remember doing a book signing in Laguna Beach, CA some years ago. It was not one of my favorite events; the owners of the new age shop had an attitude about these children, as if they could cure cancer. When I arrived for my event, I was told that I would be going on about twenty minutes late.

"Late," I said. "Why is that?" I could feel my right eyebrow rising, which is a sign that I'm not pleased.

The host relayed that there was an "indigo children's party," and that they would need a little more time.

I looked around and noticed that there were people already waiting for my lecture. They were standing around with the same impatient look that I was currently projecting. I sat down next to two women, and after eavesdropping on their conversation, I learned they were mothers of two of the children in the indigo party. I overheard one woman mention that she was very excited to learn that her son was "an indigo," and even before she could take a breath, the second woman proudly announced that her son was a rainbow child, who was much more advanced than indigo. The other mother looked heartbroken.

"Oh, give me a break," I said.

I stood up and walked outside for some fresh air and to take a moment. I sat there and thought about the damaging effects that some new age beliefs can have. Labeling kids with special titles is one of them. Talk about ego trips. Labels separate people. After another thirty minutes had passed and my reprimand about unprofessionalism had been delivered to the host, the teens opened the event room doors and began to disassemble. I still needed time to prepare the room, bless it, and get everything ready for my lecture. At the end of my talk, I offered a question and answer period.

The first question was from one of the same women I had overheard earlier in conversation. "What are your thoughts on indigo children, rainbow chil—." She did not even get the words out.

I replied with, "Horse pucky!" Of course, I explained my viewpoint with great passion that day.

The Learning Centers

Next, let's return to more legitimate matters. Once a soul passes through the veil and makes its way into the Spiritual Realm, it is welcomed by an array of support, guidance, and healing. The learning centers teach a soul what it's like to be dead. I'm reminded of the movie *Beetlejuice*, in which the couple find themselves lacking in the life force "department" after a car accident, at which time they find a book called *Handbook for the Recently Deceased*. In the learning centers, souls can choose to learn about the development of their own soul. From the beginning all the way through an unending process, souls will discover the art of creation and past lives and will relive the most important lessons from each lifetime. I'm told by my "sources" that we can travel to different lifetimes and watch our soul in action, comparable to watching a movie screen. Over time, there will be a sense of graduating from a more personal retrospective—from a "this is your life" review to a more visionary view of spiritual and supernatural truths.

Education and empowerment are essential factors for us on the earth plane as well as in the Spiritual Realm. We never stop learning. The wonderful thing there is that when we are in our spirit form, we have no mental blocks or negative beliefs hindering our spiritual evolution. It is in the Spiritual Realm that a spirit can choose to graduate to ancestral or spirit guide status. After a period of learning, the spirit can be helpful as a guide to those who are living in the physical plane. A spirit does not usually attain this status of education unless it has lived as a spiritual master, teacher, or healer for a few lifetimes. Our spiritual guides are so well informed because of what they have previously experienced here on earth.

The Healing Centers

The healing centers are locations of learning and, as expected, of healing. Well-being for a spirit is important, and understanding the dynamics of well-being takes place in the healing centers. If a soul has had great difficulty in its previous life or a death filled with suffering, it travels to a healing center for regeneration. Traumatic deaths, long illnesses, and similar issues can take a toll on the energetics of a soul, so it is here where it can rest, recuperate, and get back on its spiritual feet. Souls that have been earthbound for large amounts of time can dwell in the healing centers after successfully traveling to the spirit world. They can acquire the healing they need to recognize their spiritual selves and wake up even more fully from their deep slumber as a lost soul. The healing centers also provide sleeping chambers for souls that merely want a nice, long sleep or rest.

The Sanctuaries

The sanctuaries are very interesting locations in the Spiritual Realm. There are two uses for the sanctuaries. One use is for the binding and containment of a soul if it is a vengeful spirit, has turned demonic, or has lived a very negative and evil existence on earth. Think of it as a holding cell on the other side. When I work with exorcism and house blessing cases and run into demonic souls—souls who have over a period of time lost their light to become more of a concentrated evil, or souls with nasty attitudes—I petition the Archangel Michael. I invoke his power to bind these souls and take them to a sanctuary in the Spiritual Realm. Over time, a soul can receive ministerial counseling there and graduate to the healing centers for further rehabilitation. Demons and other beings from the Dark Realm can also be sent to a sanctuary, but I'm told by my sources that they are eventually sent back to the Dark Realm by Michael and his legions.

I did ask one time if demons can find their way back to God. The answer that I received was that all souls and all beings can always find their way back home.

Spirit Guides

Let's discuss spirit guides. The new age crowd has been interested in this popular subject for some years. No thanks to a certain celebrity psychic, for a long time most of my sessions ended with someone asking, "What is my spirit guide's name?"

I just kept answering, "Bertha," sarcastically.

Spirit guides are nothing new. Unfortunately, they turned into a fad, and the information on this subject became watered down along with almost everything else on the spiritual market these days. Spirit guides are charged by God to do exactly what their title implies, which is to *guide*. They are helpful spirits that have lived on earth for quite a few lifetimes and have had many experiences that are beneficial as guidance for us who are on this side of the veil. Spirit guides are not angels, and they do not act like cosmic bellhops. They are purely and solely helpers for our path to spiritual empowerment. If guides are worth their salt, they will always point you to listen to your own higher self. They will never direct you to listen only to them. Remember that they are charged by God to guide you on your path but not to be the source of your spirituality.

We have shared previous lifetimes with some guides, so they have chosen to help us out this time around. Guides do trade off with other guides. As children, we will have a child as a spirit guide to commune with, and as time passes, our spirit guides will interchange according to our age. When I was fifteen and began awakening as a psychic, I would see my guide who was around my age. The guide was a very strong component to my growth. On the other hand, these processes or manifestations are not written in stone. Anything with the supernatural is subject to variation. Some of us may have a guide who is young or old that may stay with us throughout our entire lifetime. It depends on the need and the empowerment of a soul.

There are different types of spirit guides and guardians, which are described below.

Human Guides

Human guides are souls that have lived human lives on earth and have chosen to become spiritual guides for us here on the physical plane. I have heard people talk about extraterrestrial guides but I feel great caution here. In my work experience, any ET-proclaimed guides have been spirit attachments with their own agendas. They are not aware of our spiritual empowerment and direction here on this planet and are not of any use for our path. That's just my opinion. Sadly, I have seen some horrible emotional and mental damage occur to many folks in new age or paranormal groups who have communicated with extraterrestrials. I believe some ETs are fine, but we have all the direction we need right here within the Spiritual and Divine Realms and on our lovely Mother Earth.

Animal Guides

Animal guides are divine archetypal energies, charged by God for our protection and influence. The animal guide or guides that are associated with us influence our lives and give us vital protection and defense when needed. In discovering your animal guide, the first clue is observing what animal or even insect is your favorite or frequently appears in your life. My husband has the spider for his animal guide. This fact does not please me since I scream like a girl around those things!

Ever since I can remember, I have *loved* ravens. Black, bold, and magical, these winged creatures have always carried a sense of mystery and sometimes the macabre for me. Some years ago—actually, many years ago now—a friend and I were visiting a local historical building in Syracuse, NY. We parked the car and took a tour of some old military locations.

Upon returning, we noticed three men with red bandanas wrapped around their heads sitting on our car. Actually, they were sitting on the hood and the trunk. We were the only ones present, and I looked around for anyone else. There was not a soul nearby but the three troublemakers and the two of us.

"Hey!" I shouted. "What in the hell do you think you are doing!" There I go again with my mouth!

I was walking toward them as though I were God Almighty. My friend tried to grab my arm and kept telling me to stop. I was not afraid of them. I continued walking toward them, not even thinking about what I was going to do once I got there. I held my gaze on all three of them. One of the bullies jumped off the hood of the car and pulled out a switchblade. I stopped and we both stared at each other. Suddenly—and I'm telling the truth—I heard ravens. We both looked up, and it seemed as though we had landed in the middle of a Hitchcock film. Seven huge ravens began descending upon the dudes, making a racket resembling nothing I have ever heard before. The three men began to run away, and I noticed that they were parked not too far from us. They ran to their car and looked back. The seven ravens landed and formed a circle around our car.

My friend caught up with me, and I could hear him say, "What the (bleep)!"

I knew that my animal guide had intervened. We walked to our car, and two of the ravens moved over so that we could enter their protective circle and get in. Once we were in our car, they picked up and flew over to the other car where the three men quickly jumped inside. Again, the ravens formed a barrier around their car. When we drove out of sight, I could see the ravens flying away in the distance. Needless to say, the three men did not follow us. I don't know what their reason was for acting like jerks, but the bullies received the treatment they deserved. All of God's children are protected.

Ancestral Guides

I wrote a little bit about this subject in the chapter about the Paranormal Realm. Ancestral guides are very different from spirit guides. Spirit guides are guiding us to our spiritual destinies, while ancestral guides seem to assist us more in our daily lives. Your ancestral guides are usually family members from previous generations who have become helpers and protectors for future generations. Working with ancestors is a very important part of many cultures. Even here in the Ozarks of Arkansas, the dead are important to many of the living. Their legacy, their meaning to those who remain behind, and even their intervention for some people are welcomed in mountain life. In my research, I have learned that while an ancestor is often that of a blood relative, within supernatural law, adoptive ancestors will also give assistance and guidance when called upon. The assistance of La Madama mentioned in a previous chapter is a good example of this idea.

You don't have to know your blood relatives in order to ask for their help. Let me be very clear about asking guides for help. With any type of guide, whether of spirit, ancestor, or animal, you are not worshipping them. They are merely helpers, protectors, and givers of wisdom. The only source to keep your eyes on at all times is that of the Creator. These spirit helpers will answer your calls, intervene, and petition the Almighty on your behalf, if needed. Sometimes when we ask God to help us, the Great Spirit sends a messenger or a helper, and we are comforted.

I'm reminded of an episode of the HBO television series, True Blood. In the episode, Sookie, the main character, battles a nasty rogue witch. To come to Sookie's aid, her grandmother returns from the Spiritual Realm to stop the witch in her tracks. After things calm down, Sookie pleads with her grandmother to help her decide what to do in life because she's afraid.

Gran replies, "Follow your heart, honey."

This scene depicts a perfect image of ancestral energy that will come to our aid and always guide us with knowledge of the heart–the truth.

Native American Guides

I'm categorizing Native American guides under the umbrella of ancestral guides. In my work, Native American guides have always carried ancestral energy. They are truly wise in the ways of the earth, herbal healing, shamanistic ritual, and just pure knowing. Over the years, Native American Indian guides seem to have been very popular for many folks involved in the new age movement. In actuality, Native

American guides have always been an important source of guidance in the Spiritual Realm. They are guardians of Mother Earth and choose to work with those of us who are truly ready to hear about her magic and mystery. Here in the Southwest, Native American spiritual leaders such as Black Elk and Crazy Horse are regarded as wisdom teachers.

In the South, we have Black Hawk. Even though Black Hawk lived and died in the Midwestern region of the United States, his spirit has lived and guided many Southerners in the ways of spiritualism. Black Hawk was a Native American Sauk and Fox tribe leader who lived from 1767 to 1838. In his lifetime, he earned a reputation as a fierce and cunning warrior who resisted governmental oppression. He also proved to be a wise leader who demonstrated great mercy and insight. Working with the spirit of Black Hawk became very popular in the twenties during the spiritualist movement in New Orleans. Spiritual leaders from the upper Midwest who relocated to the South shared the stories and legends of the very powerful Black Hawk, and soon his guidance became rooted and established with great success. Black Hawk is often summoned to help with psychic protection and liberation from oppressors. In traditional folk ways, healers and conjure doctors who work with the spiritual guidance of Black Hawk customarily place a bucket filled with earth on an altar, upon which stands a statue of a Native American Indian man. Gifts of fruit and tobacco are placed before Black Hawk, and meditation, prayers, and other offerings are made, as well.

Working with the Saints

I have been working with the Christian saints since I was a very young psychic. Even though I was raised in a rigid Southern Baptist tradition, I developed an affinity for the Catholic saints. Since I work primarily with the Christian saints, this discussion will be about them. Calling and petitioning saints for help and guidance has been a long-standing practice for centuries. If you have ever used saint cards, you will see a prayer to the particular saint on the back of each card's holy image. Saints are human guides who have walked the earth but have risen through the spiritual hierarchy. They have become spiritual guides through their works on earth as well as in the Spiritual Realm.

As in most religions, the honored dead of Christianity's holy men and women known for their spiritual devotions and miracles are referred to as "saints" or holy persons. The Catholic Church established the concept of the "intercession of saints" many years ago. This idea maintains that saints have a direct connection to God and that prayers made by them in heaven are more powerful or efficacious than prayers made on earth by regular folk. Honestly, all of us have a direct connection to God. Nevertheless, working with the saints and exemplifying their spiritual attributes can, in fact, magnify your prayers and blessings. Legendary miracles and healings connected to a saint's life made him or her the patron or supporter of certain life situations and conditions here on earth. We can ask for a particular saint's blessing in a multitude of areas in our own lives.

For example, Saint Francis of Assisi is the patron saint of birds, wild animals, and ecology. He is petitioned for the well-being and protection of all animals and for facilitating contact between deceased, beloved pets and their grieving owners. I often ask for Saint Francis's help in my healing work with animals. Images of Saint Francis show him wearing brown robes and a knotted belt. Trees, birds, and animals are frequently present in his images and represent his love for the Nature Realm. It's always helpful to have a statue of Saint Francis in your garden or green house to bless and protect your abundant growth and personal ecosystem.

Saint Jude is another good example of a powerful saint. He is the patron saint of hopeless causes or situations of despair. This powerful, divine archetypal power often surfaces at the last moment. He is often pictured dressed in green and white robes with a small flame above his head, signifying the baptism of the Holy Spirit. Again, Saint Jude is one whose aid is petitioned when all hope is lost, especially regarding health concerns or life-and-death situations. My friend Carol is a prime example of the power of Saint Jude. Some years ago I told her repeatedly that I saw Saint Jude standing beside her. It was often that his energy would be in tune with hers. She became very unsettled about this idea as she proclaimed loudly that she was not in any way a hopeless cause. What did he want with her? It was not much longer after that when Carol was busily opening boxes of books at work one day. At the time, she worked for a large corporate bookstore as a manager. When Carol opened a box of computer books, there on top of the stack she found a Saint Jude card. As God would have it, I was present for this little miracle.

She gasped and then said, "What the hell?" She picked up the card, turned to me, and said, "I'll bet you did this!"

Of course, there was no possible way that I could have interfered with a sealed box of computer books. No, this was definitely Saint Jude's accomplishment. Over time, Carol decided to connect with Jude to see what was up his green sleeve. It was revealed that Carol, who was a healer herself, was in fact someone who helped people with hopeless causes. The revelation made sense. She continually helped her family and friends with dire issues, shining a light in the darkness for them. Sometimes saints appear in order to help us, and we wind up helping them with their work, as well.

Before we leave the Spiritual Realm, we have learned that it is filled with helpful and protective beings that care about love, justice, and family. We will all be called home to this place eventually, and what a celebration that will be!

The Divine Realm

It is time to step into the Divine Realm. The veil opens to an incredible amount of power here. Angels, guardian angels, and archangels reside in this realm. The closer to the source of creation, the more spiritual power and energy will be experienced there. Spiritual masters, gods, and goddesses are archetypal powers that reside in the Divine Realm, as well. The Divine Realm shows us that there are many faces to the Source, God, or the Creator. Think of the Divine Realm as comprised of the supervisors and CEOs of the supernatural. It is here where divine guidance is given. Inspirations and spiritual knowledge flow from this realm to those who seek it. The guides from the Spiritual Realm receive their power and direction from the Divine Realm. The angelic powers are sustained by this realm for our spiritual needs as human beings who are children of the most high.

I have worked with four levels of angels during most of my professional career. Let me reiterate that I am writing about my personal experience in this book. Angels and their mission may be different for other people, but it is through my personal contact and relationship with them that I can share my information with you.

Angels are created by God and have never lived human lives on the earth. In my research or spiritual experiences, angels have never incarnated as human. They merely masquerade as humans whenever necessary.

Guardian Angels

The first level of angelic power is represented by guardian angels. Yes, we all have one. The vintage picture of an angel watching over two children as they cross a dangerous bridge symbolizes exactly what these angels do. What has upset me the most about the popular culture of angels is that some new age authors have watered down the magnificence of assistance from guardian angels to that of locating parking spaces. Nonsense! Angels do not have anything to do with our mundane life. They are guardians, warriors, and healers of our spiritual life. Our spirit guides and ancestral guides co-create with our own empowerment to assist with our physical life. Our guardian angels provide whispers of inspiration and encouragement. They keep us on our paths with intuitive direction and moments of motivated clarity. These angelic powers also govern our protection and safety. When humans find themselves in life-threatening accidents or situations and it's not their time to pass on, these angels intercede to serve and protect. Think of them as angelic police. Eventually everyone's time to cease living arrives, but before that time, the guardian angels make certain that a soul remains on its destined timetable.

Angelic Healers

These powers are healers, as the name implies. They work with doctors, nurses, and anyone in the health care area. They work with those who have the spiritual gifts of healing, as well. Angelic healers guide the surgeon's hand or empower a healer with the gift of clearing energy. Whenever friends or family members enter a hospital for treatment, I always ask an angel of healing to be with them. We can always ask for an angel of healing to work with our own power to heal ourselves, as well. Remember that angels work with us, and when asked, they can and will come to our aid for that extra push. There are angels of healing that govern all four of our human aspects—the angels of mental healing, emotional healing, spiritual healing, and physical healing. It is the Archangel Raphael that governs this angelic hierarchy.

Death Angels

Death angels sound macabre and morbid, but they are actually wonderful and interesting spirits. These beings govern transition. You have read about the Band of Mercy in this work and also in my book

Becoming Masters of Light. The Band of Mercy is a group of enlightened human souls charged with guiding lost souls to their reward. The band's supervisor is the death angel. In folklore, this force has been called the grim reaper. The Guardian of the Graves that I wrote about in the paranormal chapter falls into this category as well. Death angels protect and guard the delicate balance of transition from the physical world to the Paranormal and Spiritual Realms. We may not know it, but we pray to these angels often. When we plead with "death" not to take someone, we are directing our attention to a death angel. Death itself has always been cloaked in mystery and misunderstanding. In truth, we can write all the books we want to about death and the afterlife, but we will never truly understand those subjects until we cross the veil. Death angels are descendants of the Divine Realm but make their residence between the Paranormal Realm and the Spiritual Realm. The death angels do not communicate with humans on a "let's-chat-and-have-tea" level.

Death angels are supervisors with a mission and have no time for small talk. In ancient magical beliefs of necromancy, the death angels were called upon for the power of life force resurgence. I would not recommend this kind of work, however. The master Jesus worked with the death angels, but he was Jesus! Others of great power have been known to work with death angels as well. But again, dear readers, there are certain powers beyond the veil that simply need to be left alone.

Archangels

Archangels are the closest beings to the Creator. I have only worked with two archangels in my entire career as a psychic—the Archangel Michael, most of the time, and the Archangel Raphael, some of the time. The Archangel Michael whispered to me when I was seven years old that I would be working with him. As I grew older and became more aware of my power as a psychic and healer, I began to pay ever more attention to the role that Saint Michael the archangel occupies in our lives and the destiny of humankind. During my years as a speaker and author in the self-help and new age movement, I noticed there were many individuals who claimed to channel the Archangel Michael. He was very popular! Most channelings I encountered during that time seemed like circus sideshows. There were dramatic actions and bold vocalizations of Michael's prophecy for the planet and cosmos, and people with large egos loved to claim that Michael had chosen them as his vessel. It was tedious. One day, I decided to meditate at my altar and ask Saint Michael just what did this channeling of his presence mean. Was it true? How could he be channeling through countless humans all around the world? I lit a Catholic saint candle of Michael, relaxed, and brought myself into a deeply tranquil state. I vocalized my question when suddenly, even before I could ask the question, the answer came with a quick response.

"I do not channel through human beings." The powerful deep whisper of a voice continued. "If I channeled through a human being, half the hemisphere of the planet would disintegrate."

I replied, puzzled, and as usual got right to the point, "Then, how the hell are you talking to me?"

"Think of it like your World Wide Web; it's an email message of communication. This is a recording."

I laughed. Who knew that Saint Michael had a sense of humor?

I remembered the story of Saint Joan of Arc's ability to hear Saint Michael's voice, and thought of how he was able to communicate to her by means of an energy transference, or a divine email message.

Divine guidance comes in all forms and in many ways. Communications are all around us. We can see communication grow as ideas are exchanged through the mobile devices and Internet hubs around the world. There is a deep reflection of our own energetic and psychic communication abilities through intuition, divine guidance, and extrasensory perception. Humans have always been very gifted at creating physical devices and components that are patterned after their spiritual attributes.

I also learned from Michael that because his vibrational frequency is so close to the Source, he must be very careful entering through the veil to our physical planet for caution of matter falling apart. Saint Michael has bigger fish to fry within all the veils, and he and his legions keep the peace when needed. When Michael is petitioned for help, his spiritual legions of angelic protectors take action. They are able to pierce the veil and come to our aid on his behalf. It's awesome to contemplate or witness.

The next archangel I have worked with is Saint Raphael, the archangel of healing and restoration. His name literally means, "God heals." With Saint Raphael as with Saint Michael, Raphael and his legions of angelic healers will intercede when petitioned to help those of us in need.

When I'm performing healing vigils or seminars, it is Raphael's legion that I invoke and work hand in hand with. Raphael governs all healing modalities such as energy healing, herbal medicines, and essential oils.

Spiritual Masters, Gods, and Goddesses

Even though my foundation is Christian, I am acutely aware from all of my psychic and spiritual work that the archetypal forces of many spiritual masters and different gods and goddesses exist within the Divine Realm. Those who worship and invoke the pagan gods of old receive their direct guidance from the Divine Realm just as the Christians do. What's so interesting about the veil between worlds is that it will reflect our own deep-seated spiritual beliefs. I remember a client who called me from India and told me of her father's passing. A few minutes before he left, he raised his hand and uttered the words, "Krishna, Krishna is here, and I must go."

I knew then that no matter what your spiritual beliefs are, the veil will accommodate. Even when our beliefs are rigid and dogmatic, the veil will allow time for you to open your mind and grow spiritually. It is true that all souls at some point or another will return to God. The Master Jesus, the Buddha, the Goddess Isis of Egypt, Papa Legba, the Voodoo Goddess Oshun, and other divine powers of spiritual hierarchy in religion and ancient spiritual practices all have a platform within this realm. Think of the Divine Realm as many reflections of light that emanate from the Source, the Creator. When light hits a crystal and splinters into many directions, reflecting the colors of the rainbow, that is the image of the Divine Realm and its many faces of God.

The Source Realm

We have entered the last realm of the supernatural on our journey through the veil and beyond—the Source realm. It appears as though we are evolving upward through a spiral from the darkest of the realms to the lightest, and in essence, that's very much the case. But one thing I want to stress here is that one realm is not better than another is. I want to emphasize that all of the realms of the supernatural are necessary. Each realm is an essential reflection of a spiritual mystery that we will continue to discover more about through time. The Source Realm is the home of the Creator, the Mother/Father God, the Source of all creation, spiritual power, and magic. If we are investigating and taking a journey through the other realms, we must continuously have our intentions and our eyes focused here. The Source Realm helps us to remain grounded and to open our minds to the vast supernatural wonders that stretch before us.

I have noticed that many people in the paranormal fields try to be very scientific in their research without focusing on any kind of spirituality associated with the paranormal itself. I have found this practice to be a significant gap in their studies. When we open the door to any supernatural realm, we begin to see that there is a vast reality that is happening just beyond our nose.

The Source Realm is not a place for dogma or strict religious beliefs. This realm reflects the highest part of ourselves and accommodates our own personal view of God. No matter what spiritual path we take, the Source Realm is the same for every soul because we were created from its divine fabric. It is pure creation. As you have perused the different realms in this book, you might think that some of them are not connected to you. They appear to be other worlds to visit, and that is true on some levels. The Source Realm is not at all separate from us. It's one hundred percent within us. The Source is within our very being, pushing us higher and higher in our spiritual power to lift the veil between the supernatural and ourselves.

Over the years, I have taught thousands of people to open to their psychic ability, making sure they recognize that being psychic is an attribute of the soul and can be achieved by everyone with an open mind and heart. I am very uncompromising in my teaching of psychic study and metaphysical principles. I educate in almost a dogmatic way for fear people might fall into the trap of the bright lights and glamour associated with anything supernatural. Reality shows and self-proclaimed celebrity psychics and mediums have made it very difficult to educate folks about what are actual psychic manifestations as opposed to what is just for show or even what might be dangerous. I blame many of my current upheavals in exorcism work on the paranormal media and their misinformation about the supernatural. People will watch these shows with ghost hunting yahoos running around stirring up paranormal dust. Then, the viewers at home become cocky and try to punch open the veil, at which time I will receive a phone call because something's gone wrong. No surprise! For years I would advise folks to avoid spirit contact or divination of any kind because all I was seeing was a great deal of disrespect for these ancient tools that were being marketed as new age, inconsequential merchandise. One author who claims to be an angel expert seems to produce a divination deck every six months. *Really?* I have had friends over the years who became obsessed with their tarot cards as well as talking to the dead. I noticed that more harm than good occurred in those cases. There was a sense of selfishness in their approach to these very important occult wisdoms.

Just recently, I have softened my once rigid perception on mediumship and divination. The Source Realm, if we train our eyes to its light of awareness, can and will help us use—with respect—every supernatural tool to see beyond the veil, safely.

Using the Source to Pierce the Veil

I'm going to eat some crow here. As some of you may have read in my last book, *Becoming Masters of Light*, I was not very positive about performing divination of any kind, or even contacting spirit. The reason stemmed from my frustration regarding the lack of true education and training in these arts. In addition, the lack of respect for these ancient tools did not help my soapbox, either. As with any supernatural tool, a sense of grounding and a prayer for discernment in working with them are required. I was an excellent card reader back in my early days as a very young psychic. I was able to discover the symbols with great accuracy using my own psychic insight. Divination tools are supposed to be an extension of your own personal psychic gift. For years, I observed people using the cards without any sense of connection. It was like a parlor trick for them.

"What do the cards hold for your future?" The reality is, "Folks, what do you hold for your own future?" The cards, if used wisely, will simply reflect that truth.

Another frustration concerns keeping divination tools clear and free from outside sources that are not *the Source* within. I have always taught people to keep their tools salted for vibrational balance. Dressing your cards with holy oils is another good way to prevent negative debris. Overall, I do not want people to be disconnected from the Source within them while using divination tools in the process of spirit contact. As you have read so far, spirits from the higher supernatural realms will protect us, but they will always remind us of the source of our power. Understanding divination tools as an extension of our own Source changes our perspective completely. These tools are keys that can open doors within the veil. When we keep our sights on the Source Realm, we cannot go wrong.

The Source reminded me to allow everyone to embrace his or her own discoveries and journeys into the supernatural. I can't police the universe—no one can. We are responsible for making our own decisions when it comes to our spiritual lives. Everyone deserves the benefit of the doubt. Working as an exorcist and seeing the destruction of the Dark Realm's presence in so many cases can wear down a psychic, but keeping my sights on the Source reminds me that the light will always prevail over the darkness.

Reading about "Old Style Conjure Cards" created by an amazing conjure woman named Starr Casas really helped me to arrive at this conclusion. She recommended that when you are going to use cards for divination—hers are playing cards—make sure to use a saint card such as one depicting Jesus for the card representing the reader or the client. It hit me like a ton of bricks! The saint card used from the deck represents the wisdom, protection, and insight directly from the Source. I had never heard of this idea in my eighteen years of work with new age and psychic subjects. I think this focus on Source is an amazing process from old-fashioned divination card readings. Always hold the Source in your heart, and you will be able to lift the veil with ease. So, the next time you pull out your divination cards, use a saint card or a holy card as the central focus and foundation of your reading. That will remind you that the Source Realm—within you—is the power of your insight. Thank you, Momma Starr!

So how can we safely engage in spirit contact with help from the Source Realm? We must remember to give respect and dignity to those spirits who have crossed over or who are earth bound. As my friend Rhonda, the founder of Arkansas Ghost Catchers, says, "Ghosts were people, too." I love that. The Source Realm wants all souls that it created and all beings that it birthed to return to it one day. So all of the souls that are guided out of the darkness and into the light of awareness are progressing closer and closer to the Source Realm.

Although the Source is within us, we must remember that when we wake up on a spiritual level, we are evolving even closer to it. Life is a process of discovering our true nature and spiritual empowerment so that we can eventually return to the Source. When you are faced with any kind of spirit contact, first remember your source, and then use that power to navigate your communication, your blessings, and your direction within the supernatural realms.

Occult Tools of the Trade for Spiritual Empowerment, Ritual, and Psychic Protection

One of my favorite topics to educate people about is the reality of their spiritual power. We have the inner and outer capabilities to keep ourselves vibrationally balanced and clear of any negative energetic debris. In addition, we have the spiritual ability to shift and change, manipulate, and transform energy on countless levels. We can invoke energy when we need it. We can send energy out to others and even call it back. Your free will provides a choice about how you use your personal spiritual energy.

In this chapter, I will write about using spiritual energy for psychic protection. When those times arise where the mysterious door between worlds swings open, we can always be on guard and prepared. As with any physical situation, common sense tells us not to walk into dark alleys or in front of oncoming traffic. There is no difference in the rules regarding the supernatural realms. There are various occult tools to use within and without to keep our bodies and souls safe and in tip-top shape.

In this thrilling part of the book, I'm going to cover topics dealing with the power of thought, blessings, and curses; house clearings and holy water; sacred symbols; and more. My intention is to provide practical tools for maintaining a spiritually healthy and positive environment. I presented an excellent foundation on the workings of the inner spiritual self and the importance of the spiritual journey in my previous books, and now I will extend those truths to provide appli-

cable exercises and techniques for empowerment and psychic protection through occult means.

First, let me clarify the meaning of the word "occult." Occult simply
means anything that is secret or hidden related to the supernatural,
mystical, or magical. In this particular vein of consciousness, we are
not alluding to satanic worship or black magic as being associated
with the occult. The meaning of occult can refer to many ideas, such as
the occult teachings of Christ or the original teachings of occult medicine—or as it is called today, energy medicine. Think of occult as the
underlying knowledge of the mystical or spiritual. Occult can also be
summed up as information not comprehended by the mind or the five
physical senses; it indicates knowledge and expertise that goes beyond
the physical. The famous psychic and mystic Dion Fortune defined
"occultism" as the science and practice of working consciously and
objectively on non–physical and psychic levels. (Dion Fortune, *What is
Occultism?* [Newburyport, MA: Red Wheel, 2011]) In part, I want to help
the reader achieve this practice of occultism. This chapter resembles a
"Harry Potter, Defense Against the Dark Arts" topic. Keeping yourself
spiritually powerful is the essence and the foundation of all psychic
protection practices. As a spiritual warrior, you will need to incorporate
your newly discovered valor into your daily lifestyle. It is important to
give the same commitment to your prayer life and meditative time as
you do to your first sip of coffee in the morning. Strengthening your
inner dynamics though prayer and meditation can create a stronger
psychic armor for your mind and well-being. It's harder for negative
people or entities to disturb anyone who is tightly tucked inside a co-
coon of strength, and below are some tips for putting a shine on your
personal aura!

The Psychic Armor: The Aura

*Until the aura is pierced, there can be no entrance to the
soul, and the aura is always pierced from within by the
response of fear or desire going out towards the attacking
entity. If we can inhibit the instinctive emotional reaction,
the edge of the aura will remain impenetrable, and will be
as sure a defense against psychic invasion as the healthy
and unbroken skin is a defense against bacterial infec-*

> *tion. (Dion Fortune,* Psychic Self-Defense *[NY: Society of Inner Light/Weiser Books, 1930], 16)*

As I have mentioned in previous chapters, your physical body has what is called an aura. It vibrates from within your body through the spiritual anatomy and extends outward all the way to your arm's length. If you stretch your arms out horizontally on either side of your body, that's how far your aura reaches, especially if it is a healthy auric field. A healthy aura is powerful, bright, and colorful. If you are feeling weak or ill, the aura will condense itself closer to the body and the energy will appear more dim, faded, and murky, depending on the severity of the imbalance. We can also weaken our auric energy from reacting to life situations with fear or anger. There is power in the words, fear not! The power of our thoughts to affect our inner dynamics and outer dynamics is incredible, and learning to control that power is part of our path to spiritual empowerment. I have written extensively on the power of thought and intention in my previous books. Fear is the largest magnet for psychic attack from the outside. What we fear, we can become. What angers us will possess us if we allow it.

Thought Power

Keeping your thoughts controlled and on the positive side is the first step in maintaining a strong aura. Too many negative or untrue thoughts will weaken your energy. If prolonged, negative thinking will weaken the physical immune system as well as allow susceptibility to psychic attack or unwanted energetic influences. Sustain a holistic approach to everything in your life. Your soul, body, mind, and emotions are interconnected.

What Weakens the Auric Field
- Addictions
- Hatred
- Anger
- Fear
- Unwholesome diet
- Unforgiving and resentful state of mind

- Victim or martyr consciousness
- Sustained negative attitude
- Negative speech

What Strengthens the Auric Field
- Optimistic outlook on life
- Healthful diet
- Positive prayer and meditation
- Spiritual foundation
- Compassion
- Healthy sense of self-esteem
- Understanding yet honest attitude
- Friends and colleagues who are sensible and balanced
- Positive and encouraging language
- All-is-well attitude

Without becoming overly complicated, the simple lists posted above provide an easy way to gauge your thought system in everyday living. The task is to stay strong and positive even when your external life may be a bit rocky. Energy, people, and situations may affect us in a negative way, but how we react and perceive those outside influences will make all the difference to the fortitude of our aura's psychic shield.

What is Psychic Attack?

In my line of work, I receive numerous calls from people who swear up and down that they are being cursed or psychically attacked. In many cases, their claims are accurate. Psychic attack can happen in a variety of ways and stem from a variety of sources. It's literally a type of bullying. Psychic attack can ensue from a person who is in charge at work who for some reason wants to disempower you with words, actions, or even the abuse of his or her position. It can originate from a minister who is hell-bent on converting people to his religion by using fear and manipulation. Psychic attack happens every day on television as fear-based media and news outlets strive to enhance distress in people's lives with sensational or incorrect information. Psychic attack is a manipulation and an addiction to self-aggrandizement. It's an energy that is manifested by the deep-seated need to control, harm, and disable. Like a curse, which is an aspect of psychic attack, this energy can be conscious or unconscious. To attack or to bless is the choice we have on a daily basis. One extraordinary thing about our spiritual power is that we can defend ourselves and stop attacks in their tracks.

Spiritual Tools for Blessing and Protection

Let's learn about some useful tools that you can use in relationship to your inner spiritual empowerment. These tools will enhance your own power to strengthen and protect your auric field and environment. I use these tools myself and have shared them with clients for eighteen years. They work!

A Circle of Salt

Salt has been used for centuries as a spiritual purifier and psychic protectant. As a pure crystalline mineral from the earth, salt has the spiritual power to block lower vibrational energies and can also absorb them. I prefer sea salt—organic and raw—with no fillers. I store all my spiritual tools encased with salt. I often advise people who use tarot cards or any divination tool to add a few pinches of salt to the containers of those tools. Salt keeps the vibrational energy high, wards off any outside lower vibrations, and preserves your divine intentions. When I speak at events and subsequently visit with fans at my booth, I encircle it with a line of salt. I never know what or whom people might bring along with them—supernaturally speaking—and it's advisable to hold lower vibes at bay right from the start. Of course, I'm usually invited to speak at paranormal or supernatural events where I'm sure to run into "something," so I've learned to play it safe.

Holy Water

Water, like salt, is a powerful vehicle for psychic cleansing. It's often used for the sacrament of baptism in many religious ceremonies. The use of holy water has become famous in popular culture because of movies such as *The Exorcist* and television shows such as *Supernatural.* In the real world there are authentic reasons for this element to be highly effective in cleansing yourself and your home from energetic debris and unwanted invisible guests.

In creating your own holy water, please note you do not need a priest or holy person to pray over it to make it special. When people consult with me and I mention holy water, their first instinct is to run down to the Catholic variety store and pick some up. The creation of your own holy water is extremely powerful because your personal invocation of the Divine is infused into the water. Blessing and sanctifying your water is a beautiful ritual between you and your divinity, and no one else can perform that. It is also an incredible exercise in magnifying the use of your own spiritual power through ritual.

Making your own holy water is incredibly simple. First, you will need a glass or ceramic bowl. Stay away from plastic—it lacks good taste. Fill the bowl with a desired amount of spring water. If you don't have spring water, tap water will suffice. Add three pinches of sea salt as added protection. Again, sea salt is my preference, but table salt will work just fine. Stir the mixture with your finger a few times. Cup your hands—palms down—over the water and begin to imagine a beautiful white light pouring down from the heavens and flowing through the top of your head, down through your arms, and out through your palms into the water. The water starts to absorb the divine energy, and the blessing of the water begins. Take a deep breath, and let the image and visualization fill your mind and heart with light, ever flowing from the heavens through you, the vessel, and into your water—purifying it, empowering it, and blessing it.

If you choose, you can use the invocation here. Vocalize it three times while continuing to visualize the light flowing through your hands with cupped palms facing down.

Holy Water Invocation

Divine Holy Spirit, I invoke thee; bless this water with your protective power. May this holy water aid me in always keeping your light present. Let it aid me in the magnification of my spiritual power. And let it aid in the healing and blessing of those it touches. This water is now charged and blessed. No evil or negativity shall withstand it. I thank thee in the name of Jesus Christ. Amen.

After you have repeated the invocation three times, you may use your finger to make an outline of a power symbol (which I will discuss later in this chapter), such as the cross or the Star of Solomon above the bowl of water. Making the power symbol is like sealing the deal, and then you are finished. Pour the water into glass jars or any other containers for storage, and use the water to bless your home, holy objects, and yourself. In blessing myself, I always dab a little water on my forehead and on the tops of both shoulders. The application feels like putting on armor or being embraced by angel wings. Use the same process to bless others with holy water, too.

Let me interject at this point that I personally use Christian terms, not for religious purposes, but as a powerful spiritual source. I regard Jesus as a master magician, exorcist, and healer and the Holy Spirit as the spiritual power of God, the Divine feminine.

Salt Baths

Salt baths are a great way to keep your aura strong on a weekly basis. The salt bath is even better after a hard day's work. About once a week or as needed, fill up your bathtub. Recite the Holy Water Invocation above and pour one-half of a cup of sea salt into the bathtub. Mix, and then soak yourself from head to toe for approximately twenty minutes. After you have soaked, shower off the remaining sea salt water and allow the energy debris from the week to go down the drain. This process works wonders in giving your aura a major scrub and buff. Some people enjoy adding their own oils and herbs, as well. It's your holy bath time; throw in a rubber duck for even more enhancement and enjoyment!

House Blessings and Clearings

Now that I have covered keeping your own personal energy clear, we can discuss keeping your environment clear. It's really fascinating how our external physical life is a mirror-like reflection of our inner energetic life. We take baths to cleanse our bodies; we dust and clean our homes to make them nice and neat. We also need to use the same kind of care for our energetic fields. In cleansing your home or any location that may feel heavy with negativity (or even haunted), make certain to brew and bless some holy water as described previously. Put the blessed water in a bowl that is small enough to carry with ease. Have a second person carry a white candle. The lit candle represents the light in the darkness—the spiritual fire lighting the way and banishing any negative energy. You will want to dress your candle with a small amount of holy water, as well. Before you begin the ritual, you may want to light some frankincense and myrrh incense, allowing the incense to burn in the center of the home or in another location to aid in the clearing. Frankincense and myrrh have always been regarded as sacred. I have noticed in my own experiences with exorcisms and house blessings that that particular combination makes unwanted demonic energies run like—well, let's say run back to their hellish origin. That blend of incense is a very high vibrational combination of resin. The three wise men did not give frankincense and myrrh to the baby Jesus without a good reason!

Next, open all the windows as well as the front and back door. If you're in an apartment and the front door is all you have, just make sure it's open. Opening your space will help to move the lower vibrations, negative energies, and unwanted ghosts or entities out of your area. Trust me, when you start this ritual, negative energies will bolt out of any open door or window. At this point, your companion with the white candle that is glowing brightly and you with your holy water will be standing with your backs to the open front door, facing the inside of your location or home. Both of you will move clockwise from the left side to the right side of the entire home on all levels, if there are several present. Staying closest to your left, you will throw three pinches of the holy water in every corner while you repeat a blessing. Your companion with remain behind you, holding the brightly burning candle.

Below is my personal choice for a house blessing, but please feel free to create your own as long as it has the intention for blessing the space and banishing negative energy. Holding the holy water, you will recite the invocation aloud and your companion will follow each line of the invocation with the phrase listed below. Both of you are working together. If you don't have someone to help you bless the house, you can light a candle and let it burn in place while you wander around the home blessing and reciting the phrases. This process can be altered as long as your intentions to clear and bless the area are sincerely maintained.

House Blessing Invocation (The Lord's Prayer)

You: *Our Father God, who art in heaven, hallowed be thy name.*

Companion: *Peace be to this home (or location).*

You: *Thy kingdom come. Thy will be done, on earth as it is in heaven.*

Companion: *Peace be to this home (or location).*

You: *Give us this day our daily bread; and forgive us of our trespasses, as we forgive those who have trespassed against us.*

Companion: *Peace be to this home (or location).*

You: *Lead us not into temptation, but deliver us from evil.*

Companion: *Peace be to this home (or location).*

You: *For thine is the kingdom and the power and the glory.*

Companion: *Peace be to this home (or location).*

You: *Forever and ever, Amen.*

Companion: *Peace be to this home (or location).*

Together: *We pray this in the name of Jesus Christ.*

You will be reciting this invocation aloud as many times as you need until you go completely around the house and return back to the front door, making sure you sprinkle every corner of the house with the holy water. After the ritual is finished, place the candle in the center of the room with the burning frankincense and myrrh, and spend a few quiet moments in prayer and gratitude, letting the spiritual power take hold. I also like to light some white sage and move through the house once more as a symbolic gesture of sealing up the house with an extra measure of protection. Native Americans and other earth-based religious practitioners have used sage for many years as a blessing herb. After using the sage, you may extinguish the candle and incense. You may sense that the house's energy is lighter, now. Depending on how spiritually congested your home was, it may feel like being able to breathe for the first time without pressure or blockage. Free and clear—and blessed—home sweet home! I perform this ritual about once a month for good measure.

I have noticed that the power of this process lasts about thirty days. As life ensues, our living space is bound to cloud up with energy debris, and it will be time to chase the spirits away again.

The protective energy of the salt and holy water in relationship to your work with invocations will keep your auric energy, your home, and your personal environment safe and ghost–free. Your intention and your faith in your own spiritual power is what magnifies itself through the use of the occult tools mentioned in this chapter. All negative energies and entities will have to adhere to your personal will, as a divine child of God, to leave. Lost souls are also susceptible to your blessing and psychic cleaning techniques.

After you have blessed your home and are having a quiet moment with your lit candle, you may feel the divine energy unfold within your space. You may want to send a little prayer out to allow the light of the Divine and the Band of Mercy to help any lost souls who are stuck to find their way home to the Spiritual Realm. In my book, *Becoming Masters of Light*, I included a special invocation for spiritually cleansing your home as well as yourself. I'll include it again in one of the final chapters of this book.

Why Ritual Is Important

It is true that almost every person performs a ritual or rituals every day. For some, it's a spiritual exercise; for others, the ritual might be as simple as getting out of bed, turning on the television, and making coffee. Ritual is an exercise that is repeated for a purpose, whether it is to invoke the Divine or to brew up the French Roast. Humans have been ritualistic creatures from the very dawn of time when the first sun rose and mankind greeted the day with a prayer. There was a sense of connection between the heaven and the earth through ritual. Today there are rituals performed at churches, political gatherings, weddings, and even in Hollywood with the signing of contracts. Rituals were and are still used for initiation rites into religious organizations or special clubs. In this book, the power behind ritual is intended specifically for spiritual empowerment and strengthening your connection to the Divine. Ritual is necessary. When you are blessing your home or attending a spiritual service, you are there to magnify, transform, and embody the spiritual power that you are invoking. All the prayers, tools, and actions performed in the rituals are extensions of your own power as it connects with the power of the Divine. I have noticed that with authentic ritual there is an essential component that connects not only to the heavens but also to the earth. Water, fire, air, and earth are often used to signify that very connection. That's why I love the rituals performed by many of the earth-based religions such as the Native American or pagan practices. The connection to heaven and earth is sacred, essential, and incredibly powerful. This connection uses your entire being for spiritual empowerment and healing.

Ritual can be also used to manifest something. Affirmations are prevalent these days. Some of my friends whom I lovingly call "Love-and-Lighters" don't end a day without repeating their affirmations for abundance, love, and success. The affirmations are fine, but sometimes I observe that their rituals are more self-absorbed than spiritual. Trust me, the Divine wants us to be safe, happy, and useful on this planet. We are more likely to get what we desire by connecting to the Divine than by reciting, "Give me money!" thirty times a day with no spiritual component involved. Every ritual—from making holy water and blessing your home to manifesting something—must have a spiritual element to it. Without your authentic desire to connect to the spiritual energy of what you want, the result will always be an empty conquest. Your spiritual foundation should come first in everything you do.

Sacred Space: The Altar

By the use of invocations, prayers, rituals, and other spiritual exercises included in this book, you will support your supernatural lifestyle with strong psychic and spiritual reinforcement. It's important to set up a physical space in your home to help you focus and meditate on your spiritual foundation on a daily basis. Most people remember to pray when they visit a church or go to confession. That's fine, but creating a spiritual space in your home is something that can be of daily use. I'm not a churchgoer; my church is the sky, the ground beneath me, and the spiritual center of my being. Nevertheless, in my home, I have a dedicated room for my spiritual efforts and prayers of invocation. It starts with an altar.

You will need to create a sacred space for yourself to allow for prayer and invocation time in your life. I suggest that you create a place in your home to have an altar—a holy corner of blessing—for you to meditate or perform some of the exercises in this book. An altar in your home is a very effective way to ensure the continuous vibration of spiritual energy. This will be a space that is all your own. Here is one way that you can create a sacred space. An altar can be on a small table placed in the center or in a corner of a specific room in your home. I know that some people even use a spare closet for their altar space. First, place a specific statue or picture of a saint or spiritual master in the center of the altar. You can also place a written affirmation in the center, such as the healing words, "I am Divine Love." This statue, picture, or affirmation will be a representation of your spiritual ideal.

To be able to stand firm in your truth and your light, you must first embody a spiritual ideal in your life. Having an ideal will strengthen your inner dynamics and give you a filter for sifting away all inner and outer energies and voices. What is an ideal? An ideal is a spiritual foundation, and archetypal energy that you may invoke at any time to hold a vibration of integrity and strength. For example, many people call upon Mother Mary to assist them; Mother Mary would be a spiritual ideal by which you would measure your life. It does not have to be a spiritual master. Your ideal could be divine love, world peace, or spiritual balance. You ideal should be based in a positive light in order to keep your spiritual and physical life strong.

The main reason you want to have and embody your ideal is so that you can actually empower your mind, body, and soul with the sacred energy it represents. It's like putting on a warm coat in the winter, or turning on the air conditioner in the dead of summer. Ideals keep you comfortable and feeling secure in the elements of your supernatural life. These spiritual ideals will help you stay connected to your higher self and will pave the way for your thoughts and actions to remain in a higher vibration at all times.

In summary, your altar should reflect your spiritual self. It's a place to pray, release, re-balance, and assist with the magnification of your innate spiritual power. Remember that maintaining high vibrations is obligatory for supernatural beings that are living a supernatural lifestyle. Another important part to your altar is ensuring the presence of the elements. For example, you can light a candle for fire and incense for air. Add a crystal or stone for earth and holy water for the element of water. Placing a small plant to represent the living energy of the earth and heavens is another suitable addition. Strive for balance at your altar. Keeping the elements in harmony with your spiritual tools will help you focus on the union with the earth and the sky—as above, so below. Your meditations and prayers at your altar provide empowerment from heaven to your earthly home.

Sacred Symbols

We can use sacred symbols to enhance our spiritual power and our focus. Sacred symbols may also be useful additions to your altar space. These symbols are representations of heartfelt spiritual beliefs. Sacred symbols such as the cross and Solomon's Shield (or the Star of Solomon) are good examples. Symbols carry power. Groups of people such as church denominations, minorities, or special organizations have a symbol or symbols that represent their intention and purpose. Symbols carry the energetic representation of a group's intention. Sacred symbols, on the other hand, carry the power of the spiritual energy for which they were created.

In this discussion about sacred symbols, I'm going to use two of the most widely known symbols. These are the two symbols that are the most beneficial for my own personal and professional spiritual path. Sacred symbols placed on your altar represent your spiritual foundation. Again, I will write about two examples of many hundreds of symbols. Ask the Divine to help you find the most effective sacred symbol for you. These symbols are not only valuable for your altar but may also be worn as talismans to carry the symbolic representation of your spiritual power with you.

The Cross

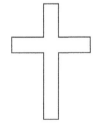

Most of us regard the cross as associated with the Christian religion. Early forms of the cross existed long before the Christian religion was developed.

In addition to the cross shown in the figure above, the symbol of the ankh cross often appeared in association with Egyptian gods as the symbol of eternal life. It's no wonder that fundamentalist Christians use the cross as their symbol of salvation and their representation for eternal life. Symbols are created and can be used with the power of the first intention with which they were created. In essence, therefore, the cross still embodies the power of life. The cross should not be regarded as a religious symbol but as a positive plus sign, instead! The cross is a sign that the universe is giving approval for your life to be lived in joy and abundance. For me, the cross is a representation of our spiritual self. It signifies the ability to overcome any crucifixion in our life and resurrect a new way of thinking and perceiving with divine love.

Pentagram of Solomon

 I'm very pleased to dispel some ridiculous myths about this symbol. The five-pointed star is not a satanic symbol! It is an ancient symbol that has been used for centuries as a representation of spiritual power and authority. In mystical Christian traditions, the five-pointed star represented the secret name of God and was worn by King Solomon as a sign of his spiritual power. In my own work with spiritual deliverance, I have experienced this symbol to be of great use in banishing heavy and negative energies.

The star represents a perfect balance of the five senses. Our psychic sixth sense at the center of the star is linked to our higher self. Similarly, Leonardo da Vinci's "Human Microcosm" beautifully illustrates a human figure with a continuous outline from the top of the head to the arms and legs and finally the spiritual center within all of mankind. You can step back and see the five-pointed star within the circle. The circle that surrounds the star is the ever-encompassing spirit of God that is protecting us and sealing us into a holy light of safety and love. I don't find it at all unusual that many of our police officers use this symbol as their protective authority.

Supernatural Powers and Protection in Southern Folklore

My great-grandfather was a healer. He was not just any healer; he was an old-style mountain healer. Legend has it that one of his "powers" was stopping excessive bleeding by simply reciting a verse from the Holy Bible. My older brother once cut his leg when he was a child. My mother told my father to run to my great-grandfather's house and tell him. My father, being the closed-minded soul that he was, hurried up to the old man's house but grumbled all the way. When he arrived, he reluctantly told him of my brother's affliction. The old man was sitting in his rocking chair on his front porch. He took a long puff from his handmade pipe, exhaled, and nodded his head. He stood up, said nothing, and walked toward his bedroom at the back of the house, picking up his Bible from the coffee table on his way. The old man shut the door behind him. And that was it. My father was not sure what to do, so he hurried back to where my mother was with my brother in her arms.

"The bleeds have stopped," she whispered.

My father rolled his eyes, and they took my brother to the emergency room for stitching. Let's just say that the ER nurses and doctor were not surprised by the healing that had already taken place in my brother's deep cut. My great-grandfather's power preceded his reputation around the little Arkansas town. My brother did not need stitches, even when all logic said he did. I believe that my great-granddaddy was an old conjure doctor—undercover.

In old-style Southern conjure and Hoodoo, the Bible is the foundation for all healings and folk magic remedies. Hoodoo itself consists of African folk beliefs with a mixture of Native American Indian botanical knowledge and European folklore. "Old Style Conjure" began in the South. Hoodoo is steeped in Christianity, which explains my great-grandfather's use of the Bible for healing. The prayers and Bible verses—along with herbs, oils, roots, and curios—make up Hoodoo.

Where I come from and still reside, the traditions of the Ozark folk magic and superstitions still seem to haunt the hills and valleys. When I was a child and coming into my own as a young psychic, no one bothered to tell me of my supernatural heritage. It was mentioned as folk tales or "just stories," and mostly in a joking manner. It was only recently when I began to investigate my past and my Ozark mountain heritage that I discovered the amazing tales and legends of magic and spiritual healings. I love to study other cultures and avenues on the subject of blessing, healing, protection, and ritual. You may find some of these practices appealing or useful for your own purposes.

I have tried these techniques or know friends who have, and they work! Remember that no matter what tool you use, the intention and the spiritual power magnified through you make it a beneficial extension for your spiritual life.

As you know, I grew up in the Ozark Mountains of Arkansas. Folklore, ghost story telling, and superstition were always a part of life with the old timers as they wove their tales of mystery and magic. My grandma was one of the most amazing folktale tellers in the hills. When I was young, she would tell me stories of her childhood and what it was like to grow up in the Ozarks at that time. There were tales of the ghostly lady in white that haunted a section of the woods just up the road as she looked for her lost lover. Grandma told about an old, abandoned house she knew of where a ghost of a man with his head split open wandered the dilapidated halls clanking his chains. To this day, you can still hear the sounds of those lonely chains and his cries. Naturally, she would tell me these stories immediately before bedtime. That was always fun! I often questioned whether my love for scary ghost stories and the macabre came from my granny. Besides telling ghost stories, I noticed that my grandmother and other old timers had some very interesting ways of life. For example, an iron horseshoe always hung over my grandparents' front door. Back then, I did not think anything of it, but in doing research on folk magic ways, I realized there was some supernatural truth to something so simple.

When I was a child, I asked about the horseshoe and why it was there.

My grandfather replied with great pride, "It's for good luck and it keeps out evil."

Okay, then, I thought, and went back to chasing the chickens. Even though my grandparents were staunch Christians, they implemented some very occult ways in their daily life. My research on iron horseshoes revealed that their significance with good luck dates back centuries. For hundreds of years, iron itself was believed to ward off unwanted spirits and evil entities. Iron has a very distinct smell, similar to our blood, and later we learned that our blood contained iron. So iron, which was crafted from the earth and able to withstand cold and fire, and which possessed a familiarity with our own lifeblood source, was looked upon with great power to withstand the unwanted supernatural effects that humans might encounter from time to time. Since ghosts and paranormal activity seem to use electromagnetic energy to manifest, in theory iron would ground the energy. As iron dissipated the electromagnetic frequencies in the environment, it would also seem to dispel spirits.

Some years later as I began to grow into my young psychic adulthood, I actually received a confirmation of the magical and spiritual attributes of iron. I love old cemeteries, and I love to walk in them. In the South, we have cemeteries that are a hundred years old or more, and the energy is quite fascinating to experience. One day, I was tiptoeing with a friend through an old graveyard in the Ozarks. It was enclosed by an iron fence that was quite bent and weathered but still intact. The entire scene would have been suitable for a sequence from the *Night of the Living Dead*. Suddenly, I came upon a young woman, a rather dead young woman. No, she was not a zombie, but she was a young girl who had died in 1888. She was sitting on her tombstone that by now was cracked, decayed, and almost completely covered over by years and years of natural debris.

She noticed me staring at her, and shouted, "Begone, devil, I'm saved! You can't harm me!"

"Contrary to what some believe, I'm no devil, my dear." I replied back.

My friend looked at me, and then looked at the invisible presence near the old headstone. She rolled her eyes and mumbled, "Here we go again." She was used to my "talking-to-the-air" moments.

"I promise you, I'm not the devil. And why are you here?" When it comes to communicating with the dead, I get right to the point; no tomfoolery for me.

"I'm waiting for the savior to take me from my grave—to heaven."

Oh, Lord, I thought. She was an example of religious, dogmatic brainwashing. These ideas destroy the mind when we're living and also carry their ugly venom into the grave.

Anna was her name, and it was etched on her stone. "Anna, have you not seen a big white light coming for you?"

"Yes, that's Satan's doorway to hell. I hide from it. I tried to run away and go back home, but I was not able to leave this graveyard. I can only get to the gate, and then I stop. I never know why. I guess preacher was right, and I have to stay here till the Lord comes for me on judgment day." She was really frightened.

With an exhausted sigh, I looked around the small graveyard and noticed the iron fence once again. At the time, it had not registered, but now I realize that there was a deep, supernatural reason why iron fences commonly surrounded graveyards. Iron was important to keep the dead inside the cemetery.

After about thirty minutes of ghost therapy, I finally talked poor Anna into crossing over. Yet again, seeing what fear does to the living and what it can do after we pass from the physical body can be overwhelming. I'm glad I went "graveyard stalking" that day. And we can now better understand the good luck that is associated with iron horseshoes.

Another interesting folk practice that I have researched and used is laying lines of red brick dust across a doorway to keep enemies at bay. History reveals that the origin of red brick dust comes from the ancient use of red ochre clay. Medicinal and ritualistic uses of this clay date back to ancient Egypt as well as to pre-historic times when cave artists used the red clay in their paintings.

On a memorable trip to New Orleans, I was invited as a special guest to the Voodoo Spiritual Temple there. It was an absolutely amazing experience. All of the dark and evil lies that I had heard about the practice of voodoo were relinquished after my chat with the temple's founder and head priestess.

"You, Boy, you talk to de spirits, yes?" She said, staring straight into my eyes—my soul, really.

"Yes, I do." I replied, in awe. What is the proper term to call a voodoo queen?

"You go! Go visit her grave, now." The queen pointed to the temple door. "Marie Laveau—she calls you. Go, Boy!" She motioned for a young African American boy to lead the way.

He walked over to me as if he walked on air—he seemed to glide over—and took my hand. As we both departed the temple, I could hear the great belly laugh of the voodoo queen behind me. *Oh, my God,* I thought. I felt like I was in an Anne Rice novel. As the young man and I walked through mysterious alleyways and neighborhoods, I noticed many of the houses had red dust that had been laid across the doorways. Some houses even had it on their window ledges. I thought about asking the young man who was my guide about it, but something told me to simply enjoy the ride. Eventually, we arrived at the graveyard where the great voodoo queen herself was buried, Marie Laveau.

I looked around and saw countless grave plots and sun-bleached tombs sitting on top of the ground; some were half-buried. Old, rusty decorative iron works and crosses dotted the place like Christmas lights on a tree. The energy was strong and very thick in this place. I was now visiting the city of the dead, according to the local flavor. Burial plots are very shallow in New Orleans because the water level is very high. It's not uncommon, even to this day, to witness a floating coffin or two after large amounts of rain have washed down the walkways of the cemetery. The rows of tombs resemble streets, and you truly feel like you're walking in an exotic village—one that's very macabre but strangely spiritual and majestic, too. After another bit of a jaunt, we arrived at Madam Laveau's tomb. Dusk was settling in and the sweet smell of magnolia breezed through the air, or was it jasmine?

It was hard to tell because I was beginning to feel like I was in a dream state at this point. The energy was very heavy—not in any way negative—just heavy, and intense. The young man who was my guide knelt at the tomb of the great lady and began to mumble words I was not familiar with in a prayerful fashion. For those who do not know, the Voodoo Queen Madam Marie Laveau (September 10, 1794—June 16, 1881), was a practitioner of voodoo and very renowned in New Orleans. Madam Laveau was famous because of her abilities and rituals and has grown to become a popular icon in this century. Today, she is looked on as a saint to those who practice voodoo and other ritualistic and magical folk traditions.

Under a sky that began to unravel its magic between light and dark, I studied the sacred tomb. Still feeling hazy, I walked closer and noticed hundreds of small, red x's and crosses marked all over the voodoo queen's tomb.

"Red clay," the young man suddenly pointed out.

I jumped, probably because I did not even realize he had finished praying. He must have noticed my investigation as I was eyeing an etched red cross very carefully.

"We use it to ward off evil spirits. We leave an offering for Madam Laveau and she blesses us with her healing and protection."

I looked down and noticed flowers, pictures, and other trinkets placed everywhere around the tomb. At the time, I was wearing a smoky quartz bracelet. It was my favorite, but something in me wanted to leave an offering.

I felt I was drawn to her tomb to deepen my own understanding of ancient spiritual ways that carry truth. Perhaps the great voodoo queen was the catalyst for this experience. I left the bracelet at the tomb, with thanks, and the young man led me back to the lights of Jackson Square—back through the veil and into the land of the living.

Do folk magic remedies and rituals carry power? Are they myths? I know there is a true power of the root, or the spirit. After my experience in New Orleans, a friend of mine named Sal put the red brick dust to the test. He owned an organic food shop, and he had decided to fire a disruptive employee. She had bragged about being a witch and how she was going to curse the place. In my humble opinion, the girl did not have enough spiritual juice to pump a bicycle tire, metaphorically speaking. For weeks, the girl's cronies would come into the store and snicker, case the joint, and leave. Soon my friend began to notice the disappearance of items after these groups of girls would hover and then leave the store like shadows. After the shoplifting continued for a few more weeks, I jumped in with the idea of laying down some red brick dust. My friend laid the dust at the front and back door, with a welcome mat to cover the magical evidence. *Ironic*, I thought.

A few days later, Sal noticed a familiar old jalopy of a car pull up in front of the store. Out stepped a few of the girls from the guilty party. This time, the girl he had fired was with them. There were three girls. They walked up to the door and stopped short. Sal watched one of them put her hand on the door to open it, and then she gradually backed down as if in slow motion. The two other girls also seemed glued to their positions outside of the door. Sal could not believe what he was seeing!

Suddenly, the girl he had fired popped out of her daze and said, "Screw this place, I'm not coming back here."

They retreated and drove off, and Sal has never seen them litter his doorstep again. So, was it the dust? Was it Sal's power of intention? Does iron stop spirits in their tracks? Will holy water wash evil away? Will salt protect you from vibrational harm? Are all of these ideas merely hocus-pocus? I'll let you be the judge, dear reader. Try something and see for yourself. I believe that every ritual, spiritual tool, and prayer are fueled by our intentions. The spiritual power behind each method is its combustion to work. Whether we use a rosary, an iron horseshoe, or red brick dust, our spiritual power can activate properties in these tools to assist our psychic protective armor. Crystals, herbs, stones, and oils are readily accessible tools for our healing, protection, and well-being. This world within the veil and the spiritual energy behind it have so much to teach us. Ancient practices and the evolving consciousness of the present day can offer an amazing marriage of spiritual intelligence.

Never be afraid to learn, grow, and discover what's out there for you—spiritually. The Divine will protect you all the way. The best safeguard of all is knowing and embodying the truth that *you* are a child God, and nobody will mess with that!

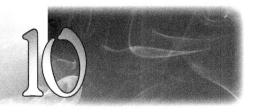

Prayer Practices through Petitions and Invocations

As many of my readers know, all of my books come well equipped with prayers and works of invocation. I'm including something new in this book. It's actually not new; it's a practice that is older than dirt, and it works. I have started using the ancient practice of petitioning, and it is truly a spiritual eye–opener. I now understand where many of the illustrious teachers of *The Secret* and *The Law of Attraction* acquire their ideas. They have fluffed up these ideas with plenty of love and light, but in this chapter, we will discuss the root of petitioning. There will be an added bonus of more prayers and invocations for you to use on a daily basis. I believe that much of what we call new age thought has been commercialized and bastardized from the old folk ways of spiritualism, as well as from the ancient practices of ritual magic and invocation. I will briefly describe (from my own spiritual point of view) what prayer, petitions, and invocations are, and then I'll explain how to use the spiritual power attributed to all three. I'll give you samples to work with so that you will be ready to write your own spiritual prayers from your heart. It is important to understand that all three of these tools for spiritual practice work together and are very similar. Some people believe that there is no difference, but I'll let you be the judge.

Petitions: Prayer Work from a Southern Folk Wisdom Perspective

Spiritual petitions are one of the oldest forms of prayer work—they are found in the Holy Bible as well as in other holy texts. The word petition indicates a written prayer or formula that seeks to create a specific, desired outcome or blessing. In the old folk and hoodoo belief systems, petitions are essential to the practice. For those of you who are not familiar with the practice of hoodoo, let me clarify here. I wrote a little bit about it in the last chapter. Hoodoo, also known as rootwork, is Southern folk magic enriched with African American spiritual flavors; Native American Indian herbal knowledge; and Ozark, Appalachian, and Southern folklore beliefs. Hoodoo is known by other names including conjure (which is my preference), rootwork, root doctoring, working roots, or "doing the work." Hoodoo is not a religion; it is a spiritual magical system. What's fascinating to me is that the majority of root workers are Bible-based Protestant Christians who pray the Lord's Prayer and recite the Psalms. Hoodoo practitioners are called by many names including conjurers, conjure doctors, root doctors, root workers, or two-headed doctors, which is a reference to the relationship between the practitioner and his spiritual guide. As related in the previous chapter, I have a renewed fascination in researching this practice after learning that my great-grandfather was a conjure man. I have discovered some great spiritual truths in this practice, and petition work is one of them. I believe that petition work truly improves your hands-on experience with the Divine and is much more meaningful than empty prayers of pleading and begging. I have always taught that prayer is a two-way street and must be a practice of merging the Creator with the one who is praying.

In the old days, petitions were written on brown paper similar to that of a paper bag. Paper bags were easily accessible to people who might be poor, lived in the hills, and also practiced old style Southern conjures and healing work. "Fancy paper," in most cases, was not available or affordable. Nowadays, we know that a petition is a formal, written request appealing to authority—in this case a spiritual authority—with respect to a particular cause or outcome. Petitions generally need to be written on a balanced piece of paper where the sides are equal. It is thought that the balance is what helps direct the energy of the desired outcome.

I personally like to use brown paper in memory of the old practitioners of long ago. I'm going to give you a simplified version of this practice, and for more in-depth study, please refer to the folk magic book recommendation at the end of this book. A petition is written about what you want to attract, bless, prevent, or protect. Remember that a petition acts as a specific desire to be helped and influenced on your behalf by the Divine. As you write out your petition—through affirmation or request—you are giving specific directions about the help that you want from the spiritual powers. The goal of a petition is to create a change in a situation concerning yourself or someone else. This practice is a wonderful tool for sending a blessing or for ensuring psychic protection. There are many and various ways to write petitions, but I prefer a simple but powerful form of this practice from the Southern Old Style Conjure method. The forerunner in that area is Starr Casas. In Starr Casas's wonderful book, *The Conjure Workbook Volume 1: Working the Root*, she shares her views on petition writing:

> *When I write out my petitions I always date and sign it. You need to make sure your intent is clear. Here's an example of what I'm talking about. Let's say I need a job. If I write my petition out and state "I want a job." Or I want a job doing (Whatever). Then I'll get just a job. I may hate it, and not get along with my co-workers. But what if I change the wording of the petition like this*
>
> *Date:*
>
> *Birth:*
>
> *Name:*
>
> *I want a job doing _____. I want to make more than enough money to make ends meet (or place the amount you want to make). I want to be comfortable with my new boss and the people I work with. I want to be seen as a favorable asset to the company. I want a raise within _____ amount of time. I want this to be the perfect job for me.*
>
> *Signed_____*

([Sunland, CA: Pendraig Publishing, 2013], 269-70)

We can see from Momma Starr's, as I love to call her, example that we must be specific in our petitions to the Divine. Whether we are asking about love, money, work, or the need for a spiritual blessing, we must focus our intentions. See how this idea is reflected within the Law of Attraction craze? We can largely give thanks to the conjure and root work methods that have been around for hundreds of years for the teachings and application of intention and co-creation. The reality of our ability to co-create with the Divine itself is a timeless truth. Learning to manifest, create, and direct power—and use it wisely—is essential. This ability is becoming more and more apparent with the lifting of the supernatural veil. As we lift the veil beyond, we lift the veil from our spiritual eyes, as well, and we begin to see just how powerful we really are as divine beings.

The Spiritual powers want us to work with them, and the Source of all creation has set many guides and guardians to help us. They want us to focus our attention and intention on our higher self and will help us to work with our spirituality for the benefit of healing, justice, and well-being for ourselves and others.

When I write out a petition, I like to place it on my altar. The placement of my petition seated on a powerful saint card or under a specific candle helps to empower its spiritual energy. If you are looking for justice in your life, place your petition on your altar with a Saint Michael statue or candle. Petition his fine justice on your behalf. You can write out the petition to Saint Michael, and by placing it on your altar dedicated to him—trust me—he will get the message! Pray at your altar every day, not in desperation, but in sweet surrender, and rest assured that you are being cared for. Use the same method for healing. A statue of Jesus or the Archangel Raphael, along with your petition for healing, may be placed on your altar.

This process helps you to have a hands-on experience with your prayer and altar work. It is no longer an empty task of asking for divine help. Instead, you are working an authentic process and literally calling in the Divine by ritual and faithful dedication. One thing to remember is to constantly maintain a clear intention. Despite all of our prayers and petitions—and for the new age believer, their vision boards and affirmations—there is a spark of creative magic that we are trying to generate and embody. The Source is always watching out for you and has your best interests at heart. The key is to keep your discernment intact and your intention to co-create with the Divine fully open and strong.

The Power of Invocation

Invocation is another powerful tool of prayer. I use it often in my exorcism and healing work. I use petition work for my everyday needs, and I work with invocations for more spiritual and psychic needs. Invocation is the highest form of prayer. All of us can use our spiritual power if we believe and have enough faith in the power within us to use it. In my work, invocation is a calling forth of an inner spiritual power to achieve a healing, a blessing, or some protection. As we use petitions to saints and ancestral guides to aid us, we can also use the power of invocation from the angels and the Holy Spirit to increase our blessings and our own psychic protection.

My previous book, *Becoming Masters of Light*, is filled with healing formulas and invocations. For this book, I promised you my full, unedited invocation for spiritual protection. I decided to water it down a bit in the previous book so that it would not shock too many souls about the reality of negativity, but I think you can handle it now. It's important to realize that your intention and your spiritual power are what actually propel the energy to work with any kind of prayer efforts. If you pray or petition with a sense of complaint or victimization, the spirits do not respond to that weakness. They like to see you shine in your power. The Creator made you powerful, so start acting like it! That's the first step in achieving results on any level from this work.

Invocation for Discernment

Holy Spirit, wash my physical eyes and my spiritual eyes clean. Let me see truth beyond all illusion. Let my intuitive and psychic power be strong and always at the ready. I see through the Light of God, and all darkness falls away. In the name of the Father, the Son, and the Holy Spirit. Amen.

Invocation for Spiritual Cleansing and Protection (full, unedited version)

This invocation will help to access powerful spiritual protection. As a child of Mother/Father God, you are always under the Creator's watchful eye and can call on his or her protection at any time. By invoking these divine archetypal energies, you will feel not only safe and secure in your world, but you will realize that the Divine will always take care of you. Spiritual protection is accessed from within you. As you *vocalize*, the *Christ* vibration and presence will begin to expand, and the lower vibrational entities and energies will begin to loosen. The lower vibrations will be forced to release their attachment to your personal energy field. This invocation can be used whenever it feels necessary for you. Some people like to use it at least once a month for healthy spiritual maintenance.

Invocation for Spiritual Cleansing and Protection

Band of Mercy, I invoke thee. Please remove all lost souls and unclean spirits that may be attached to, affecting, or influencing me (or for another person, insert the name), my family, my house, my pets, my property, and all that I have domain over, and place them in the appropriate sanctuary or do whatever you deem necessary. I ask this in the name of *Jesus Christ*, and I thank thee. Amen.

Angelic Protectors, I invoke thee. Please remove all negative entities and energies that may be attached to, affecting, or influencing me, my family, my house, my pets, my property, and all that I have domain over, and place them in the appropriate sanctuary or do whatever you deem necessary. I ask this in the name of *Jesus Christ*, and I thank thee. Amen.

Archangel Michael and your legions, I invoke thee. Please remove all negative entities, demonic beings, the djinn, and any other adversarial energies, thought forms, and influences that may be attached to or affecting me, my family, my house, my pets, my property, and all that I have domain over, and please place them in the appropriate protected sanctuary or do whatever you deem necessary. I ask this in the name of *Jesus Christ*, and I thank thee. Amen.

Archangel Raphael and your legions, I invoke thee. Please balance and restore my energy anatomy and auric fields. Please seal and heal all negative psychic holes, vortexes, channels, rips, and all remaining energetic traumas in my energy body. I also request this healing for my family and my pets. I ask this in the name of *Jesus Christ*, and I thank thee. Amen.

Holy Spirit, I invoke thee. Please guide and protect me. Please dissolve and disperse any and all remaining fearful, negative, or residual energies, and replace them with your unlimited light, love, and grace. I also request this protection for my family, my house, my pets, my property, and all that I have domain over. I ask this in the name of *Jesus Christ*, and I thank thee. Amen.

Definitions of Terms

Band of Mercy: *The Band of Mercy* is comprised of enlightened souls that are assigned to assist those who have died to pass into the Divine Realm. Since the souls in the Band of Mercy are ministers and healers, they specialize in the careful transition of souls that are lost or earthbound through the light. The essence of their work is in making the transition of souls between worlds as easy as possible.

The Archangel Michael: The Sword and Shield of God. *The Archangel Michael* and his legions help in the removal of negative energies and entities on this earth plane. Michael is also summoned for protection and strength during times of immense fear, chaos, or confusion.

The Archangel Raphael: The Lord of Healing and Restoration. *The Archangel Raphael* and his legions help us to restore, heal, and balance our energy bodies and chakra systems. He also guides us in our own healing practices and therapies.

The Holy Spirit: The living breath of the Mother/Father God. *The Holy Spirit* is the anointer of wisdom, grace, spiritual awakening, and pure Divine Love. The word holy means "whole," and spirit is equivalent to "being." So, the Holy Spirit can be thought of as a force pushing all existence toward wholeness. When this energy is called, it helps sustain balance and restore peace, bringing wholeness back to the individual or a situation. The Holy Spirit "seals the deal" and envelops you in the protective power of Divine Love.

Jesus Christ: Master of Masters. *Jesus Christ* is the supreme ideal for spiritual enlightenment and the master exorcist and healer.

Sanctuary/Protected Sanctuary: *A Sanctuary* is a special clinic located in a dimension between this earth plane and the Divine Realm. It is used to heal and restore souls who suffered traumatic deaths, long illnesses, or deaths by suicide. Once ready, the souls can continue to the Divine Realm. *A Protected Sanctuary* is a type of multidimensional holding cell for lost souls who require restraint. Its purpose is to bind a variety of demonic beings from doing any further harm. Ministering, salvation, and healing are also offered here.

Invocation for the Blessing of an Altar

Divine Holy Spirit, Ancestors, and Protective Guardians, I invoke your power and presence. Please bless this sacred altar with your wisdom and your spiritual altar works. May the intent of my prayers and blessings always be directed by your guiding hand. Surround my altar with the holy light of awareness, cleansing, and protection. For it is here that I dedicate my spiritual self and my work to your good intentions. In the name of *Jesus Christ*, I thank thee. Amen.

Invocation for the Blessing of the Ancestors

Divine Ancestors whom I have known or not known, I invoke thee. By the power of the Holy Spirit, may your wisdom and insight guide me in all my ways. You are my wisdom–givers and protectors, and I am forever blessed by your presence in my life. May your power open all paths, doorways, and avenues to abundance and healing in my life. And to you I will always bestow gifts of honor and respect. In the name of *Jesus Christ*, I say this invocation with right intention, and I thank thee. Amen.

Invocation for the Release and Deliverance of a Lost Soul

Dear and loving soul who has lost your way between worlds, I invoke the Holy Spirit's light on your behalf. You will find light within the darkness. Come Holy Spirit, help to free the chains and shackles of this earthbound spirit. Help this soul to see your light and open its restlessness to your care and comfort. Go home, dear soul, cross over, and be forever blessed by the light of God. Know that you are safe and secure—no longer lost, but found. In the name of *Jesus Christ*, I thank thee. Amen.

Invocation to Banish Evil and Demonic Influence

In the name of Jesus Christ and all the saints, by the power of the Holy Spirit, and by the protection of my ancestors, I banish you, evil spirit. You are not welcome in my home or in my being. Begone, by the power of *Jesus Christ*, and be cast back from which you came. I invoke the Archangel Michael to aid me in my safety. As a child of the Most High, I have the spiritual authority to banish you, evil one. By the power of Christ, begone! Amen. (Repeat three times.)

Final Notes on the Supernatural

So here we are, dear reader, at the end of this particular journey. I think—no, I *know*—that this is the book that has actually helped me to grow even more while writing it. To finally feel the spiritual liberation of putting my experiences down on paper about such a mysterious and elusive topic is almost too overwhelming for words. I feel a great passion and desire for people to see the supernatural not as a world far beyond but as a world that exists all around us. The supernatural is very close to our own lives and surrounds us on a daily basis. We are, in a sense, supernatural ourselves. The fact that we pass through the veil at birth and at death gives us a close encounter to that which brings wonder, magic, and wisdom.

While writing this book, I returned home to the Ozark Mountains of Arkansas, which I left behind twenty years ago and to which I thought I would never, ever return. "Never say never," as they say! And I have never been happier in my life. Through all of my interactions with reality on this physical plane and also at the crossroads of the veil, I have learned so much as a spiritual, God–loving soul, and as a human being who simply exists day–to–day. The acts of discarding my self-made constraints, accepting my empowerment, and remembering who I really am have opened doorways that I thought would never budge. Seeing the magic and the folk wisdom from my Ozark Mountain sanctuary has been a true revelation unto itself.

When I was a kid growing up in the small town of Mountain View, Arkansas, my experience was very different from what it is like now to live here as a seasoned adult. As some of you may have read, my young life was a very painful time for me. Living in a small town plus being dirt poor provided a perfect reason for me to leave, experience

new places, and grow; but somewhere along the way, I realized that
my happiness was my own responsibility. It was not the fault of my
childhood that sent me packing, although it was the slingshot for my
journey. I had to leave and be lifted by a cyclone of adventure as well
as a particular passion to learn more about life. I like Dorothy's quote
from *The Wonderful Wizard of Oz*: "If I ever go looking for my heart's desire
again, I won't look any further than my own back yard. Because if it
isn't there, I never really lost it to begin with."

After twenty years of supernatural wonder, I'll never get over the
supernatural *natural* wonder I discovered right here at home. In researching more about my Ozark homeland and ancestral heritage, I've
discovered stories and legends of healers and folk magic practitioners
galore. I was not ready for this awareness as a child and had to take my
spirit's journey. When the time was right, I was ready to click my heels
and return home where all the answers and power were all along.

I'm starting to understand why I have been so sensitive to the veil
between worlds. It's in my blood. The magic and mystery of the supernatural are in your blood, as well. Taking a step back from the physical
world and focusing on what's vibrating behind it might be just the
kick-start you need to discover the answers to your questions and your
prayers. All wisdom comes from the Source, and all you have to do is
remember the power and the magic that you were born with. Embrace
it, live it, respect it, and love it; and you will pierce the veil to realize
a deeper meaning in your life and your destiny. One day, all of us will
travel through the veil for the last time and return to our true home,
the Source. And we will all celebrate the truth in declaring, "There's no
place like home."

Recommended Reading

Angels and Demons

Brittle, Gerald. *The Demonologist: The Extraordinary Career of Ed and Lorraine Warren*. Los Angeles: Graymalkin Media, 2013.

Davidson, Gustav. *A Dictionary of Angels: Including the Fallen Angels*. New York: Free Press, 1994.

Guiley, Rosemary Ellen. *The Encyclopedia of Angels*. New York: Checkmark Books, 2004.

———. *The Encyclopedia of Demons and Demonology*. New York: Checkmark Books, 2009.

Cryptid Creatures and Interdimensional Beings

Blackburn, Lyle. *The Beast of Boggy Creek: The True Story of the Fouke Monster*. San Antonio, TX: Anomalist Books, 2012.

Guiley, Rosemary Ellen. *The Djinn Connection: The Hidden Links between Djinn, Shadow People, ETs, Nephilim, Archons, Reptilians and Other Entities*. New Milford, CT: Visionary Living, 2013.

———. *Monsters of West Virginia: Mysterious Creatures in the Mountain State*. Mechanicsburg, PA: Stackpole Books, 2012.

Gerhard, Ken. *Encounters with Flying Humanoids: Mothman, Manbirds, Gargoyles & Other Winged Beasts*. Woodbury, MN: Llewellyn Publications, 2013.

Ghosts and the Paranormal

Fiore, Edith. *The Unquiet Dead: A Psychologist Treats Spirit Possession*. New York: Ballantine Books, 1995.

Guiley, Rosemary Ellen. *The Encyclopedia of Ghosts and Spirits*. New York: Checkmark Books, 2007.

———. *Rosemary Ellen Guiley's Guide to the Dark Side of the Paranormal*. Milford, CT: Visionary Living, 2011.

Nature Spirits and Faery Folk

Eason, Cassandra. *A Complete Guide to Faeries & Magical Beings*. Newbury-port, MA: Weiser Books, 2002.

Foxwood, Orion. *The Faery Teachings*. Arcata, CA: R.J. Stewart Books, 2007.

———. *Tree of Enchantment: Ancient Wisdom and Magic Practices of the Faery Tradition*. Newburyport, MA: Weiser Books, 2008.

Southern Folk Magic

Casas, Starr. *The Conjure Workbook Volume 1: Working the Root*. Sunland, CA: Pendraig Publishing, 2013.

Foxwood, Orion. *The Candle and the Crossroads: A Book of Appalachian Conjure and Southern Root-Work*. Newburyport, MA: Weiser Books, 2012.

4TH DIMENSION PRESS

An Imprint of A.R.E. Press

4th Dimension Press is an imprint of A.R.E. Press, the publishing division of Edgar Cayce's Association for Research and Enlightenment (A.R.E.).

We publish books, DVDs, and CDs in the fields of intuition, psychic abilities, ancient mysteries, philosophy, comparative religious studies, personal and spiritual development, and holistic health.

For more information, or to receive a catalog, contact us by mail, phone, or online at:

4th Dimension Press
215 67th Street
Virginia Beach, VA 23451-2061
800-333-4499

4THDIMENSIONPRESS.COM

Who Was Edgar Cayce?
Twentieth Century Psychic and Medical Clairvoyant

Edgar Cayce (pronounced Kay-Cee, 1877-1945) has been called the "sleeping prophet," the "father of holistic medicine," and the most-documented psychic of the 20th century. For more than 40 years of his adult life, Cayce gave psychic "readings" to thousands of seekers while in an unconscious state, diagnosing illnesses and revealing lives lived in the past and prophecies yet to come. But who, exactly, was Edgar Cayce?

Cayce was born on a farm in Hopkinsville, Kentucky, in 1877, and his psychic abilities began to appear as early as his childhood. He was able to see and talk to his late grandfather's spirit, and often played with "imaginary friends" whom he said were spirits on the other side. He also displayed an uncanny ability to memorize the pages of a book simply by sleeping on it. These gifts labeled the young Cayce as strange, but all Cayce really wanted was to help others, especially children.

Later in life, Cayce would find that he had the ability to put himself into a sleep-like state by lying down on a couch, closing his eyes, and folding his hands over his stomach. In this state of relaxation and meditation, he was able to place his mind in contact with all time and space—the universal consciousness, also known as the super-conscious mind. From there, he could respond to questions as broad as, "What are the secrets of the universe?" and "What is my purpose in life?" to as specific as, "What can I do to help my arthritis?" and "How were the pyramids of Egypt built?" His responses to these questions came to be called "readings," and their insights offer practical help and advice to individuals even today.

The majority of Edgar Cayce's readings deal with holistic health and the treatment of illness. Yet, although best known for this material, the sleeping Cayce did not seem to be limited to concerns about the physical body. In fact, in their entirety, the readings discuss an astonishing 10,000 different topics. This vast array of subject matter can be narrowed down into a smaller group of topics that, when compiled together, deal with the following five categories: (1) Health-Related Information; (2) Philosophy and Reincarnation; (3) Dreams and Dream Interpretation; (4) ESP and Psychic Phenomena; and (5) Spiritual Growth, Meditation, and Prayer.

Learn more at EdgarCayce.org.

What Is A.R.E.?

Edgar Cayce founded the non-profit Association for Research and Enlightenment (A.R.E.) in 1931, to explore spirituality, holistic health, intuition, dream interpretation, psychic development, reincarnation, and ancient mysteries—all subjects that frequently came up in the more than 14,000 documented psychic readings given by Cayce.

The Mission of the A.R.E. is to help people transform their lives for the better, through research, education, and application of core concepts found in the Edgar Cayce readings and kindred materials that seek to manifest the love of God and all people and promote the purposefulness of life, the oneness of God, the spiritual nature of humankind, and the connection of body, mind, and spirit.

With an international headquarters in Virginia Beach, Va., a regional headquarters in Houston, regional representatives throughout the U.S., Edgar Cayce Centers in more than thirty countries, and individual members in more than seventy countries, the A.R.E. community is a global network of individuals.

A.R.E. conferences, international tours, camps for children and adults, regional activities, and study groups allow like-minded people to gather for educational and fellowship opportunities worldwide.

A.R.E. offers membership benefits and services that include a quarterly body-mind-spirit member magazine, Venture Inward, a member newsletter covering the major topics of the readings, and access to the entire set of readings in an exclusive online database.

Learn more at EdgarCayce.org.

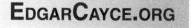